Paul Smith
A to Z

PAUL SMITH in conversation with OLIVIER WICKER

Abrams, New York

He wanted to become a professional cyclist; today
he is a world-famous designer. He left school a
fifteen, and now heads a global company with more
than three thousand employees. Paul Smith is a
fashion designer who is not a megalomaniac, and
who is not temperamental or obnoxious to his
colleagues. He has never been in detox, does no
travel in a private jet and has lived with the same
woman, his wife Pauline, for forty years. Is he a
regular guy? Not exactly. His shops are filled with
very stylish suits, little metal robots and porcelain
rabbits. His London office—a chaotic space filled
with thousands of books, a robot collection and pink
bicycles—is a housekeeper's nightmare. He is likely
to show up at dinner wearing mismatched socks . .
        More than eccentric, Paul Smith is a
creative force with his feet firmly planted on the
ground. He is a man who is never without his
camera, who will drop everything to photograph
a particular flower or a passerby and who will
stop in his tracks, mesmerised by the colour of a
seventeenth-century painting. At the same time
he can quote the exact production cost of a T-shir
or the price of a yard of a particular fabric
For many designers, the process leading up to
the launch of a new collection is complex. The
Paul Smith approach says a great deal about its
namesake. He starts with dozens of photographs
taken during his trips, along with entire folders
of Post-its scribbled in hotel rooms, with such
sentences as "Inspiration is everywhere" or "Life is
a puzzle." His words, images and thoughts are ther
brought to life by his design staff, and eventually
transformed into the clothes that will be sold
in his shops. For more than thirty years, he has
never lost his touch, and his sensibility continues
to seduce his clients. Sir Paul Smith's mind may
follow strange pathways, but it always reaches
the finish line. Paul Smith has a theory about Pau
Smith: He believes that his dyslexia (discovered
during his childhood and never addressed) prevents
him from thinking in a purely rational manner. His
brain is not formatted for linear thinking and is
constantly interrupted by thousands of ideas

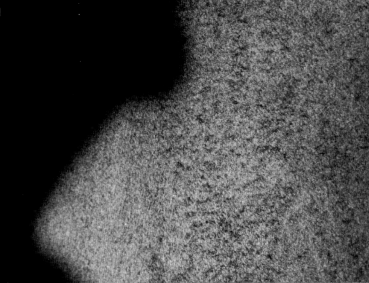

He has, in fact, retained the soul of a child. This long-haired man may head a well-known global company, but he remains curious about everything. Neither his popularity (especially in Japan), nor his creations or style, cool and chic at the same time, are about fame. Paul Smith is interested in people: Working people or members of the royal family, rock stars or students, he listens to them all. This attitude sets him apart from the zoo of egos that make up the majority of the fashion world. Self-taught, he never lost control of the company he created, and he earned the respect of his clients. Many fashion houses have relinquished control of their businesses to financial groups. Paul Smith refused to listen to money's siren call. He remains as independent as he was when he opened his first shop in Nottingham, and continues to do as he pleases. Taking a two-hour train ride to attend a rock concert, hopping on a plane to visit the Great Wall of China to return the very next day, putting on a show in Korea displaying the gifts he received over the years from an anonymous sender . . . None of this is difficult for him. Quite the opposite, since he gets his best ideas on the run: The smallest detail of an image can inspire next season's collection.

For many years, Paul Smith pointed his camera toward buildings, flowers, faces, Japanese food displays, and unexpected situations, like those captured by his friend, Martin Parr.

To illustrate this book, the first in which the designer explains, literally from A to Z, who he is, where he comes from and what makes him tick, Paul Smith and I have selected from among thousands of his personal images. It seemed a perilous task at first, but within a few days, proceeding as he does, by association, he organised images and words in an order that is his own.

Leafing through the pages of this book, it is clear that Paul Smith is much more than a gifted clothing designer: He observes the world through an extra-large prism, while still zooming in on the most minuscule details—poetry in the moment.

—Olivier Wicker

A for

Abbey Road

The Beatles on Abbey Road. That was 1969. I had already been sharing my life with Pauline for two years. She is from London, so we often went to concerts there, and of course, saw The Beatles. The atmosphere of those days was all about originality and freedom.

A for
....

Anquetil (Jacques)

When I was twelve years old, Jacques Anquetil was my
idol. One day, as I was talking to my father about this
racing cyclist, he said: "Djackenktiiil? What does
that mean?" My parents had never left England
and had no idea what this man represented
to me, with his five Tour de France vic-
tories. In those days, media coverage
was not as it is today, so I knew
nothing else about him, and
I imagined his life as
totally heroic.

E MIROIR
ES SPORTS
présente :

4
GES

POUR ANQUETIL, LA

1.5
N. F

de

LYETT-FYNSEC

DOUCE DES RÉCOMPENSES : LE BAISER DE SA FEMME JANINE

GRAHAM WATSON'S
TOUR DE FRANCE T
ITALI
two wheels
BRIAN HOLM DEN SI
THE FULL CYCL

GIT

A for

Architecture

I lack both the intelligence and the technical qualities to be
a professional architect, but have always been fascinated by
the subject. I like the language of architecture—how you
need to express the rhythm of a building, its proportions,
how it connects to its environment. In fact, conceiving
an architectural project is a little like designing a jacket:
You need to find the right balance. I have tremendous
admiration for Carlo Scarpa, an Italian architect who
chooses his materials with extraordinary precision. He
will select a specific type of wood for a certain place,
stone for another . . . that makes perfect sense to me.
I have noticed that more and more cities are making daring choices in their architecture in order
to attract more tourists. It's a good thing. As I
design the interiors of all my new stores, I
imagine how their volume will fit within
the city, how people will move around
inside the space. Five years ago, after
consulting with Mexican and Italian builders, I opened a shop in
Los Angeles that was inspired
by the work of the architect Luis Barragán. Imagine a huge California-pink shoebox, right on
Melrose Avenue. Inside, the mood is warm,
intimate, slightly disorganised (even though
I see a very personal sense of order there).

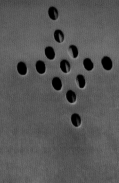

I don't think of my work as art, and I am often disappointed by art and the conceit and arrogance of many artists. They take themselves too seriously and develop their own language to feel important. Fortunately, no one understands what these people are saying. I find this interesting. I don't agree when people refer to my work as art. It would be better to speak of creativity, which is at the centre of what I do. The actual idea and the communication of this idea, its development and realisation, are creative processes. You need to find the perfect balance among all these energies, which is not always easy. Also, in the contemporary art world, many artists become famous and successful one day, only to fall into obscurity the next. In the 1990s, artists were very involved in networking, promoting themselves through that medium; they wanted to shock. I don't have a problem with that; it's just not my way of working. If you don't like someone's work, you can simply zap it, as you would on television. If people annoy you, don't speak to them; speak to their cat instead.

A for

Art

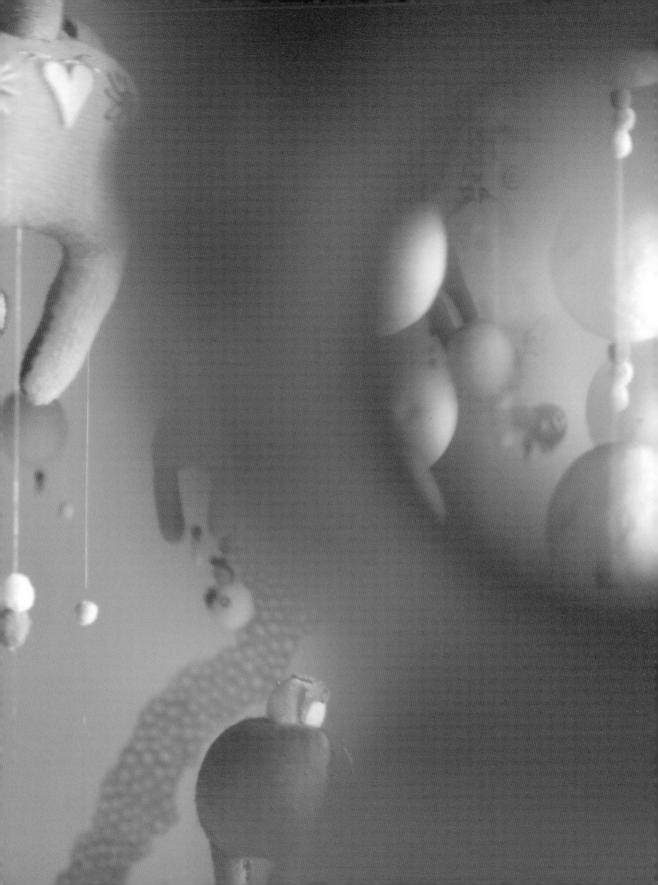

B for

Best (George)

I met this amazing footballer from Northern Ireland. He is immediately recognisable by his sideburns and his taste for champagne. His story is that of a superbly gifted person who succumbed to depression. He made an enormous amount of money, but did not have the right people to advise him financially. The women who went out with him did so for the wrong reasons. He suffered a great deal while many people around him took advantage of him. His story reminds me of rock stars who become famous when they are very young, can't deal with their success and end up drowning in a swimming pool.

« # SMART
FROM THE
START »

Boss

One thousand people in Europe and two thousand in Japan work for Paul Smith Ltd. To find balance within a company, I realised that you have to ask questions before giving orders, even when there is disagreement over a specific detail or a global strategy. In the end, you always reach a solution that satisfies the largest number of people. I learned this when I consulted with a kind of psychiatrist. I met with him only twice, twelve years ago, when I was struggling with my women's collection. He explained to me that the issue was not about gaining X's trust or agreeing with Y, but to work with them to find a balance that would assure a satisfying result.

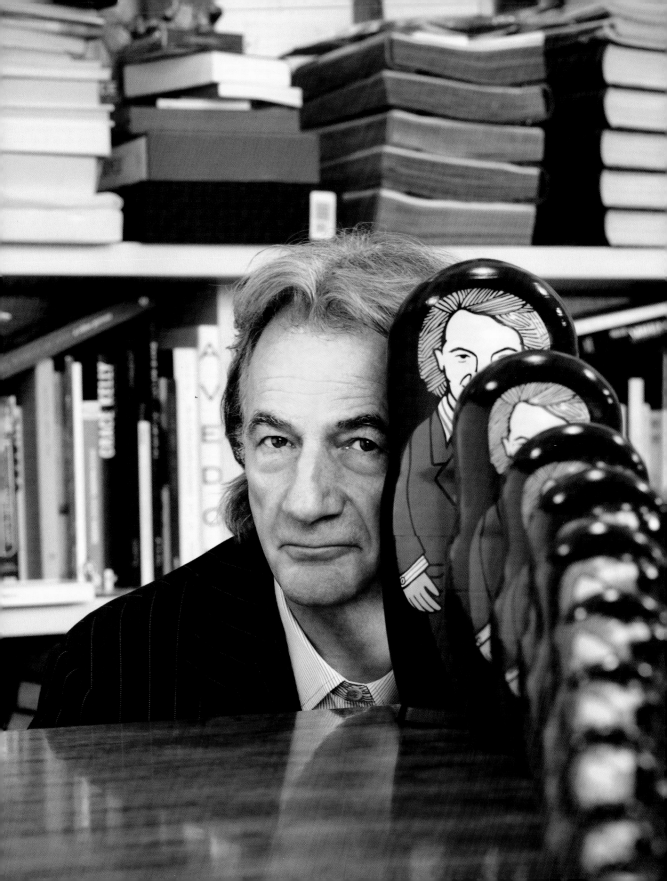

B for

Bowie (David)

His first album [*David Bowie*] came out in 1967, the year I met Pauline. That is the reason why we have seen him in concert so many times. Before him, British radio only played jazz from the 1920s. Bowie's androgynous looks were not meant to be irreverent; they were simply innovative. In May of 1968, the French youth movement expressed its frustration with protests and political battles. Here in England, the anger was expressed more individually, for example, by one's look; we are probably less politically engaged than the French. His concerts at the time, such as Ziggy Stardust [in 1973], reached great heights. Everything involved in the production—the music, costumes and staging—was incredibly coherent. The atmosphere was electrifying. I also had the chance to see The Rolling Stones perform in small venues; it was more intimate and experimental. There were no rules then. Today, when fifty thousand people attend a concert, everything is calculated to the millimetre.

In 1981, I saw David Bowie again at a privately arranged concert where he sang "The Party's Over." I finally met him in 1982, at a private auction at Christie's in London. He told me he was a great Paul Smith fan; you can imagine how much that meant to me.

B for

Brand

I hate the word "brand." Throughout the world, my name is a brand. But this disturbs me. The word encompasses aspects that displease me. In the world of fashion, it symbolises all the nonsense of the past twenty years: the über-celebrity of models, the excessive spending and the burden of financing. Paul Smith is a different kind of brand: We are not part of a big group, we have no five-year plan and we do not spend our time having strategic marketing meetings.

I started my business with Pauline, my wife. We never borrowed any money. I own 60% of the company, and my Japanese shareholder owns the rest. Many offers were made, but I like being independent.

I remember, in the 1990s, when the big groups were taking over: Fendi, Céline, Gucci . . . You would typically hear a designer say: "Oh dear!! I have an enormous problem! I am becoming too popular, too commercial. It's terrible!"

As for me, I have more of a working-class attitude; my natural inclination is to spend as much time with the porter who takes out the rubbish as with a rock star.

From left to right: Paul and Steven Berkoff, Paul and Michael Palin, Paul and Alan Aldridge, Paul and Albert Watson, Paul and Blake Mycoskie

Paul and David Tennant

Paul and HRH the Duke of York

Paul and Sarah Miller

Paul and Henry Holland   Paul and Grayson Perry

Paul and Patricia Field

Paul and Jonathan Ive   Paul and Luciano Benetton

Paul and Mika

C for

Celebrities

Paul and Paul Weller; Paul and Joan Burstein

Paul and Lady Diana; Paul and Sam Taylor-Wood

I have yet to use the face of an actor or actress for my publicity campaigns. Since the start of my career, I have followed one rule: I want someone, somewhere, to want to buy what I make because he or she likes that particular suit or shirt or dress and not because it is associated with a celebrity. It's my way of doing business.

Paul and Mark Cavendish; Paul and Craigie Aitchison

Paul and Jack Newling; Paul and Johnny Borrell

Franz Ferdinand; Paul and Tre Cool of the band Green Day; Paul and Ricky Wilson of the band Kaiser Chiefs

Paul and Jamie Oliver

Paul and Taj Forer

« I LIKE THE UN-EXPEC-TED »

C for Club

We live on a planet where people do not feel safe. Sometimes, I have the strange feeling that people choose to belong to clubs to feel safer. Having a card, mingling with other members and having the same conversations can give one a sense of security. This, in turn, will necessitate other possessions. Mobile phones and computers, tools that are very practical, are often used obsessively by many of my contemporaries. Most people who use a mobile phone are hooked on sending daily text messages. While I have no hostility toward technology, it is simply a question of balance. When people drive and are riveted to the GPS device, they will look at a 3D representation of a museum on a little screen when the actual building is right there in front of them.

I am not a collector; I just accumulate a large quantity of the same items. In my mind, a collector is someone who will spend hours talking to you about a particular lamp that was designed in 1890 by a certain obscure designer, and about the fact that only eight others exist throughout the world.

People who make things fascinate me. How does the process work? How did the idea come to them? And how did they make it? From all the things accumulated in my London office, one idea will form

Collector

and be the inspiration for a collection or for the design of a new shop. For example, I can combine two different shades of pink that I see on a book cover or a plastic robot and realise that this would be the perfect shade for a women's shop, all pink with shiny doors and matt walls. This kind of idea will hit me at any given time. It's strange and sometimes hard to describe, it comes and goes, but it's never a burden. And I never say to myself, "Wow, what a great idea!" The process of production is as interesting to me as the inspiration.

In the 1980s, when conceptual art was in style, I thought, "So what?" For me, talent and happiness come from turning an idea into reality. That's brilliant. Having ideas is the easy part.

« I LOVE LIFE »

C for

Customers

I left school at fifteen. When I was
eighteen, I helped a friend start a
clothing shop. I quickly learned what it
meant to get up early to open the shop, deal
with clients and close the door late at night after
straightening everything out. Paying rent, and, if
possible, paying yourself . . . I learned about all of that
very quickly. Many designers who attended prestigious
fashion schools never had that experience. When I founded my
company, the business structure was still very basic and I could
handle it on my own. I remember keeping records in a ledger
that was called "simplex" because it was, in fact, simple. The company grew, and John Morley, a man of great courage, became
Managing Director; the success of Paul Smith is due in great
part to Morley. Thanks to him, I was able to focus on designing
clothes and developing the "brand."

I have attended many dinners with highly educated people.
I am self-taught, so I have devised a way to not be intim-
idated: As I sit down, I tell myself that they are like
anyone else; they go to the bathroom, and that as
children, their mothers changed their nappies . . .

a bad student, and never passed a single exam. been tested, but I have known since I was very am dyslexic. There is a certain pride in belonging famous dyslexics, I have never sought treatment. ords very well, and when I write, I always forget a ak in public, which happens often, I need to have ad, since it's impossible for me to read my notes. work with do not understand how my mind kly, how, as a dyslexic, I can solve five or six prob me time. I actually think that my hyperactivity is this "pathology," this handicap that is not really n does not follow a linear path. It moves quickly, itous way. I think "laterally," which is enormously you do creative work. I have never met anyone as I do, Jonathan Ive, for example [who designed Apple], does not understand how I function. I direct answer to a question. . . . My team has had to the strange ways of my brain.

D for

Dyslexic

I was always a bad student, and never passed a single exam. I have never been tested, but I have known since I was very young that I am dyslexic. There is a certain pride in belonging to the club of famous dyslexics. I have never sought treatment. I can't spell words very well, and when I write, I always forget a letter. If I speak in public, which happens often, I need to have it all in my head, since it's impossible for me to read my notes. The people I work with do not understand how my mind works so quickly, how, as a dyslexic, I can solve five or six problems at the same time. I actually think that my hyperactivity is connected to this "pathology," this handicap that is not really one. My brain does not follow a linear path. It moves quickly, but in a circuitous way. I think "laterally," which is enormously helpful when you do creative work. I have never met anyone who works as I do. Jonathan Ive, for example [who designed the iPod for Apple], does not understand how I function. I never have a direct answer to a question . . . My team has had to get used to the strange ways of my brain.

Some famous dyslexics:

Hans Christian Andersen
Nathalie Baye
Marlon Brando
George Bush Jr.
Prince Charles (and his son Harry)
Cher
Winston Churchill
Tom Cruise
Walt Disney
Thomas Edison
Edward VII
Paul Ehrlich
Albert Einstein
Dwight D. Eisenhower
F. Scott Fitzgerald
Gustave Flaubert
Benjamin Franklin
Zsa Zsa Gabor
Galileo
Whoopi Goldberg
Stephen Hawking
William Hewlett
Dustin Hoffman
Anthony Hopkins
John Irving
John Fitzgerald Kennedy
Robert Kennedy
John Lennon
Leonardo da Vinci
Magic Johnson
Steve McQueen
Michelangelo
Wolfgang Amadeus Mozart
Nicholas Negroponte
Jack Nicholson
Louis Pasteur
General George Patton
Edgar Allan Poe
Robert Rauschenberg
Nelson Rockefeller
Auguste Rodin
Paul Smith
Steven Spielberg
Sylvester Stallone
Richard C. Strauss
Ludwig Van Beethoven
Jules Verne
Robbie Williams
Thomas Woodrow Wilson
Henry Winkler
William Butler Yeats

Last week, as I was heading for the bathroom in a café, I realised that I was wearing one mauve shoe and one black shoe. Luckily, they were the same style.

E for

Eccentricity

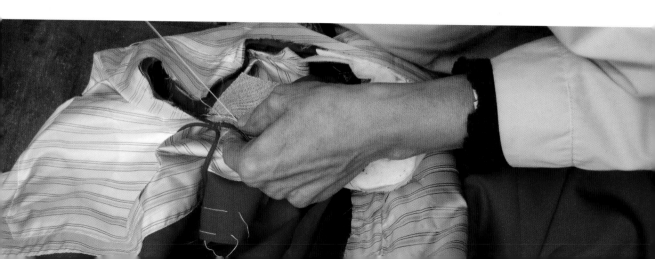

E for

Evening classes

A high point of my career [*laughs*] … When I started out, I took evening classes, once a week, with a tailor. I learned that every detail is important, that modifying the cut by just a few centimetres can completely transform the shape. Mainly, I retained that a well-cut garment can give anyone an elegant look, a stronger aura. Those evening classes were not the most glamorous period of my life, but remembering them keeps me grounded.

EVERY **I** DAY, **GET** IDEAS

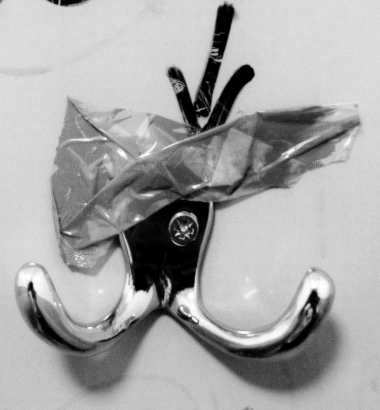

F for Fashionable

Having style and being fashionable are two different things. With the right attitude and personality, you can have style without having money. Being fashionable is a more complicated exercise: You need to be up to date on everything and have financial means. I believe that people who are addicted to fashion are seeking reassurance. In my daily life, I would not say that I dress "fashionably"; my style is *casual,* but I do appreciate beautiful clothes and the feel of fine fabrics. Which brings us to the word "dandy." A dandy is a type of man who has practically disappeared from the planet. A true dandy thinks about the suit he will wear the next day. His choice will be based on what he has worn the previous days, his schedule, his appointments and the weather. Then, the shoes, tie, fragrance . . . It's a full-time job that few can sustain in today's world.

F for
....

Fashion
....

show
....

As soon as a fashion show begins, all I want is for it to be over so that I can go and have a drink.

I am not a big fan of fashion shows, but they are part of the theatre of fashion. No one has found

a replacement for this ritual that serves brands so well. The show is the final ingredient of a recipe

that's been on the stove for six months. I am much more interested in finding the key idea and

choosing the fabrics and colours. At that exact moment, I can already visualise the clothes that

will reach the stores six months later.

F for

Father

I always believed that
my father could have
done many of the things that I
have. He was always even-tempered,
always approachable. When I was a boy,
home sick with the flu, I heard a noise outside
my window: There stood a creature made from a
sponge mop with a hat and eyes . . . My dad was trying
to make me laugh so that I would feel better. Other times he
played "flying carpet." After school, he would sit on the living
room carpet and pretend to be flying to exotic countries. He
was a door-to-door salesman who sold, on credit, all the latest
household products, including fabrics for the home. It was a
typical post-war job: Everyone was short of money and bor-
rowing was commonplace. He saw customers every day. His
most remarkable trait was his practical sense. He did everything
at home: painting, electrical work, car repairs, fixing the
roof . . . My dad kept a list of all the things that fascinated him. His lists were often surreal, like a list of
the world's ten longest rivers. He was always
very elegant. Even at the age of ninety,
when he was housebound, my dad
always chose his shirts and ties
with great care.

TAKE PLEASURE
SERIOUSLY

F for Flowers

During the 60s, many young men got in touch with their feminine sides. Designers began creating floral-patterned fabrics for men; previously, men had only worn solid-colour suits. Flowers were the symbol of the late 60s and early 70s, of Led Zeppelin and Pink Floyd. They are a recurring pattern in my collections that appear randomly on ties or scarves . . . They are my discreet homage to the concept of freedom that characterised that era.

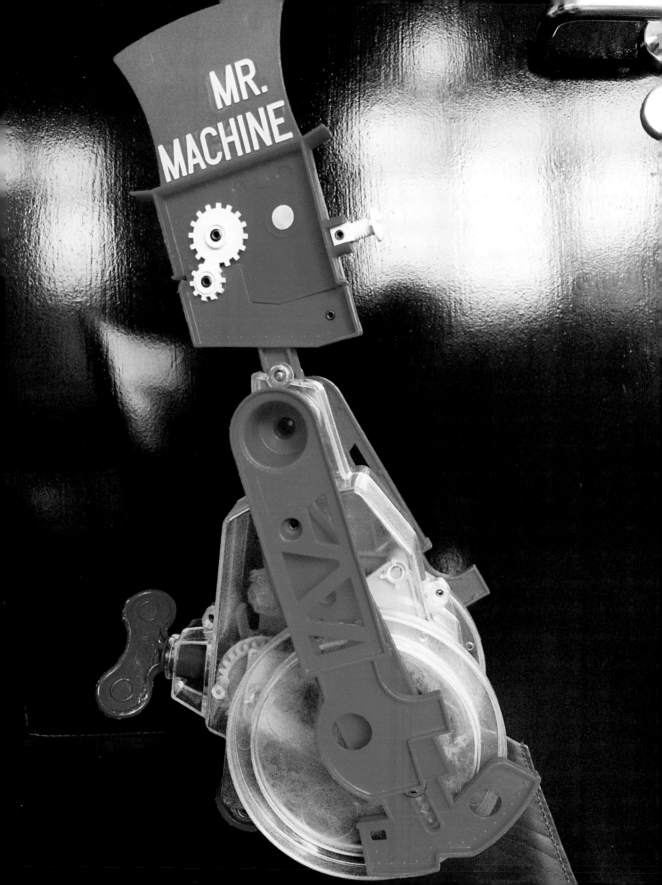

When I went to Japan for the first time in 1982,

I discovered dozens of gadgets that could not be

found anywhere else. I always brought back a selection

of them for our shops where they sold out immedi-

ately. They attracted many different types of clients,

such as architects and designers. That gave birth to

the idea that modern clothes and gadgets could

be sold side by side. In a world already filled with

objects, I like the idea that some people con-

G for

tinue to create new things that can fulfil new

Gadget

functions. Conversely, the idea that the

same objects can be reproduced end-

lessly and take over our lives frightens me a little. A designer recently

told me, "I need to design a new coffee machine every year to maintain

a sense of newness." I wonder if this frenzy will ever stop.

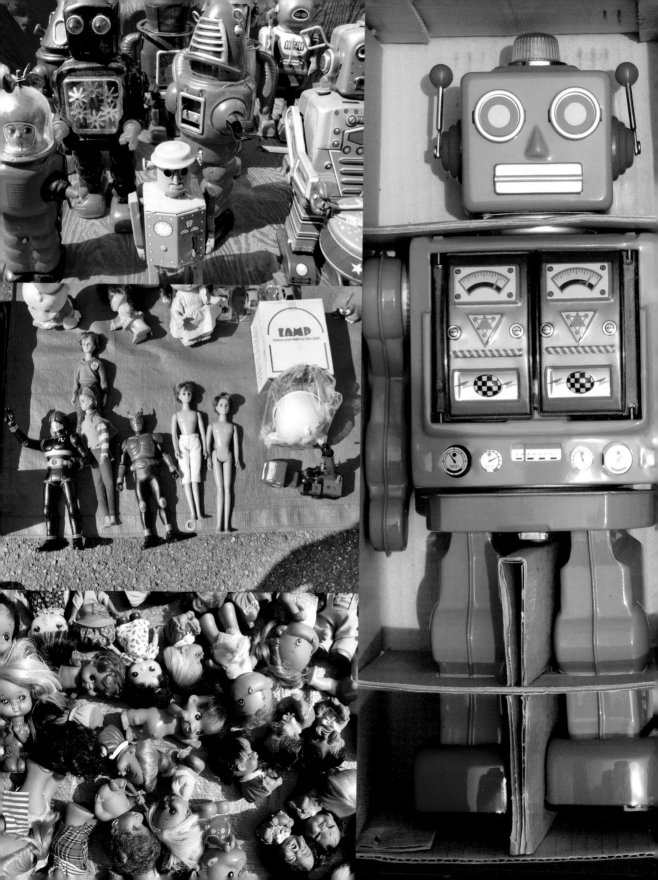

« FASHION
IS NOT
ABOUT
YES
TER
DAY »

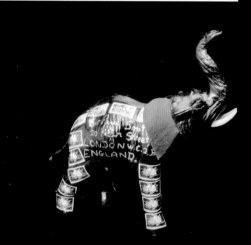

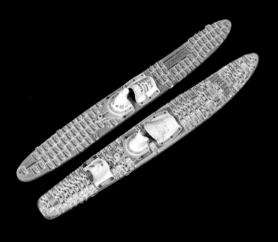

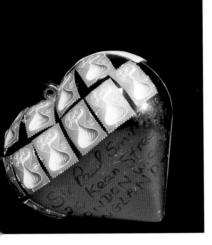

G for

Gifts

Over the years, and from all over the world, I have been given many fantastic objects that end up working together: posters from Africa, pink bicycles, ceramic rabbits, dozens of little robots and hundreds of books. And then, there are all the letters. Recently, I received a very moving letter from an eighty-four-year-old woman who is dying of cancer. In her letter, she wrote about her daily trips to the hospital for her chemotherapy treatments and how much wearing the Paul Smith "Rose" perfume had helped her. It touched my heart. I also received a letter from a ten-year-old girl who was doing a school report about Paul Smith. A few years ago, a young boy asked me to design a T-shirt for his hamster named Rupert. I personally answer all these letters. I don't know why people write to me, but I think I was born with a gift for communication. I am very grateful for this ability because it comes to me naturally.

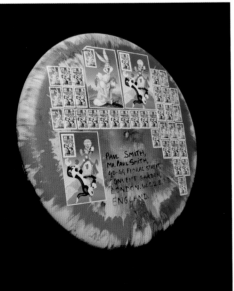

H for

Hotel rooms

Wherever I travel, I always reserve the same hotel room. In Tokyo, it's always room 4250. That way, when I wake up, a little jet-lagged, I can always find the light switch and my way around the bathroom. I do the same when I go to New York or Paris. I also eat the same thing most of the time; that way I don't need to think about it too much. This kind of organisation and repetition stimulates my imagination. I invent games based around this "routine." Recently, instead of waiting for the elevator in my Tokyo hotel (my room is on the forty-second floor), I decided to run up the stairs. The game had two points: Count the number of steps to reach my room and try to beat the elevator. I lost on the second point. That's the sort of inane thing my dad would have done.

I recently had to have a CT scan. It was nothing serious, but everyone (patients, medical staff and my own team) was concerned that I was going to be locked inside a metal tube for thirty minutes. As it turned out, I actually felt very relaxed inside the machine, even while the doctor kept asking me over and over again if I was all right. I was not aware of time passing; I just let my mind float and drift toward ideas, drawings and colours.

I for

Inspiration

"Inspiration is all around us" is one of my favourite phrases. In the colours of an eighteenth-century painting or in the graffiti on a wall . . . To keep track of my sources of inspiration, I use a camera that I keep with me at all times. It's for my "visual diary."

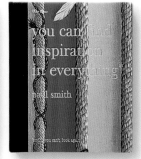

FOURNIER STREET E1
LONDON BOROUGH OF TOWER HAMLETS

No parking
outside this
gate in
Constant Use

I for

Ive (Jonathan)

Jonathan Ive designed the iPod, iPhone
and iPad for Apple. I have the greatest respect for
his inventiveness. The shape he created was both archaic
and totally futuristic. When he came to my office for the
first time and saw the chaos in which I work, he was amazed
that such disorder could be a source of inspiration for me.
Often, I can find connections among all these objects: The
pink colour of the bicycle will remind me of the pink shade
of a dress in a Martin Parr photograph; those two tones
might be the colour of my next shirt . . . Getting back to
Jonathan Ive (even this explanation is dyslexic!), he invited
me to give a talk on creativity at the Apple offices. I was
shocked by the amount of secrecy that exists within the
company. To reach a certain conference room, you must go
down a specific hallway so that you don't happen to come
across a new product. I told the Apple engineers—without
any notes because I am incapable of reading them—that
you can be more creative by freeing your mind rather than
encumbering it with useless information. In exchange, I
received an astonishing gift from Jonathan: a giant iPod
that was almost my size. I have not yet checked to
see if it actually works.

I have been going there since 1982. I felt welcomed immediately, probably because I did not behave like other Western entrepreneurs who were there only to make money. At the time of my first visit, my company consisted of six people. I barely had any money and my first contract with Japan didn't bring me much revenue, but it was consistent. In Japan, I learned about teamwork. At each meeting, there were always four people present who did not speak; they just listened. All the designers I know who went to Japan in the 1980s, when Japan became a fashion destination, complained of the time difference, the food, the culture that

J for

was so different to theirs. I travelled in economy class, without limousines or fancy hotels. The Japanese have a radically different approach to business. Their thinking is "you win, I win." Both sides work together toward a common result, whereas we Westerners have the tendency to take without sharing. Most of the designers who expected to profit from Japan's economic boom of the 1980s are no longer working there. I think that I touched the heart of the Japanese. I offered my friendship, and I was interested in their lifestyle and values. Slowly, I learned to listen and speak to them.

Japan

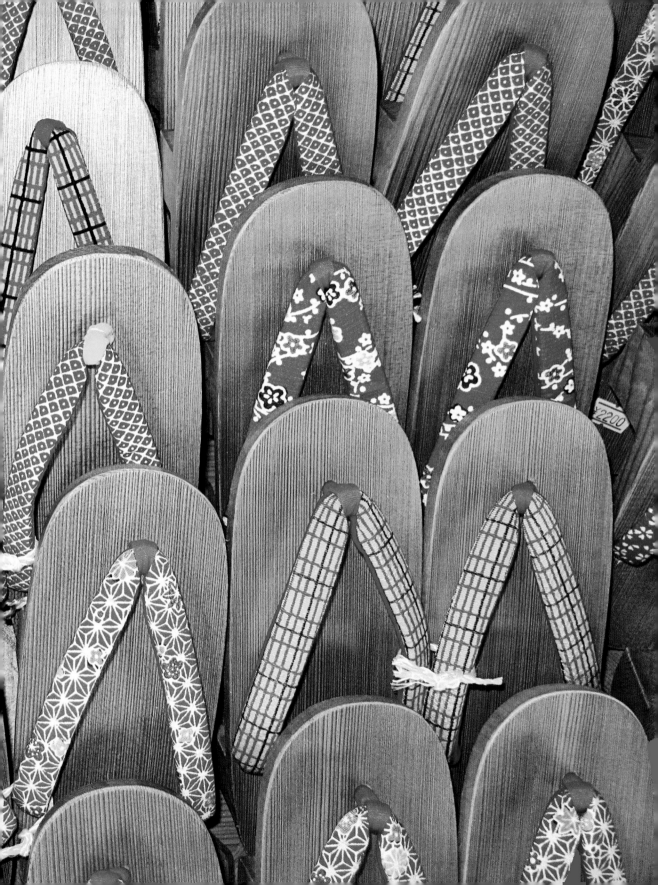

L for

....

"Logic" is a mysterious word. I can't tell if I am relentlessly logical
or if my mind functions in a completely illogical way. Many of
those around me would suggest the second option. Still, I see
things very clearly   and find that many
                                            people talk in very
                                            convoluted ways
                                            about topics
                                            that are very
                                            simple.

Logic

....

L for

London

L for

Love

I always pay attention to the points of
view of others. I am not "in love" with the
people on my team, or with humanity in general, but I am fascinated by the fact that there
can be thousands of viewpoints on the same
subject. A friend recently gave me a T-shirt that
had the letters L, O, V and E on it, but he had
modified their order to spell VELO [bicycle].

M for .... *Merckx (Eddy)*

He is another one of my cycling heroes, in the same amazing league as Anquetil. He made me dream. The recent doping incidents have somewhat tarnished the sport, but nothing could keep me away from the Tour de France.

M for _____

Pauline and I started the business together. We never borrowed any money and still don't. I am the majority shareholder. I like

being independent and making decisions as I see fit. I have turned down many offers from big companies who wanted to buy

Money

ours. The members of my team had a hard time understanding my decision, and I decided to draw up a study to evaluate what we

stood to lose. They finally understood, but the explanation was an expensive one!

I was born in Nottingham, and my parents spent their entire lives there. My sister still lives in their house. I opened my very first shop in Nottingham when I was twenty-four years old. The shop measured three metres by three metres. There was no window, and clients had to walk through a hallway to reach the store. The two or three customers who came in each day were met with the warmest welcome. For the store's décor, I went to little shops that sold Art Deco pieces and mixed them with posters that I found in art galleries or brought back from Paris, where Pauline and I went with other design students. When people came into the shop, there were many things to look at besides clothes. The tight space created a warm and friendly atmosphere. People came ready to buy. We started off selling only men's items. Some customers came from miles away.

I loved the responsibility of setting up the shop, running it and welcoming the customers. If I could earn a living from one shop, I wondered, would having two or more shops eventually change me? I would have to make some compromises along the way. This idea still haunts me today. I tell students not to neglect the commercial aspect of business. It really helped me to learn the balance between business and creativity.

N for **Nottingham**

In 1976, when Pauline and I started the small Paul Smith collection, we managed all aspects of the business. I found the fabrics and the manufacturers; we were handling the sales and even made some pieces ourselves. We were able to balance design and marketing. Today, when I meet with my team, we know we also need to make decisions such as whether a certain item will be sold at Bon Marché or elsewhere.

The premise is always the same: When you come into a Paul Smith shop, even if you don't buy anything, it should be a pleasant experience.

O for

Observation

Many people around me do not see what I see.
I am not boasting about it; it's the way I was born.
The observation of daily life is an amusing exercise.
Finding absurdity in everyday life is a very British tradi-
tion: Alan Bennett, Mr. Bean and Monty Python are great
examples of this, indeed. British humour relies heavily on tim-
ing. In a formal gathering, you must be respectful and extremely
polite before casually making an outrageous remark. Every
day of my life, I witness something that makes me burst
out laughing.

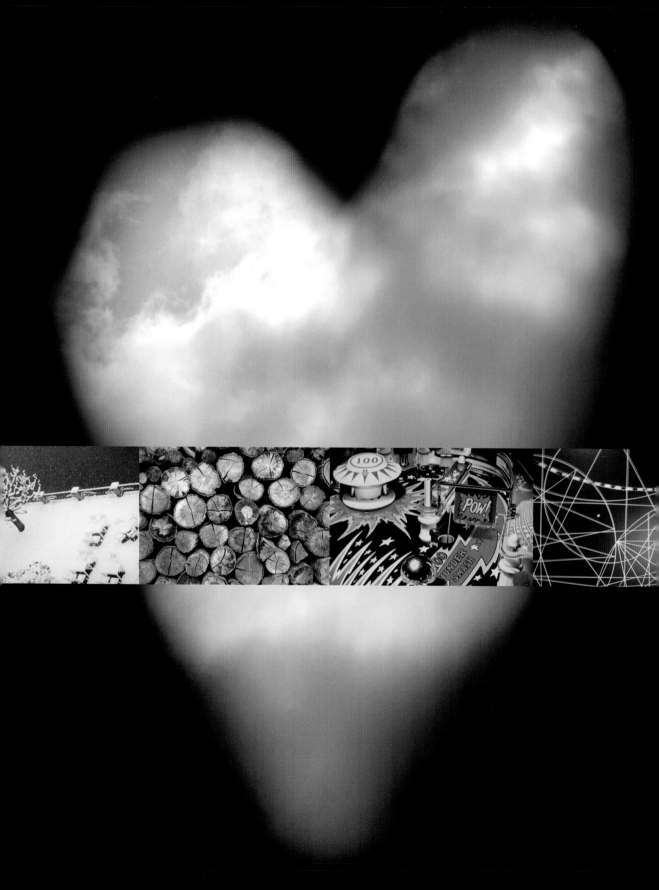

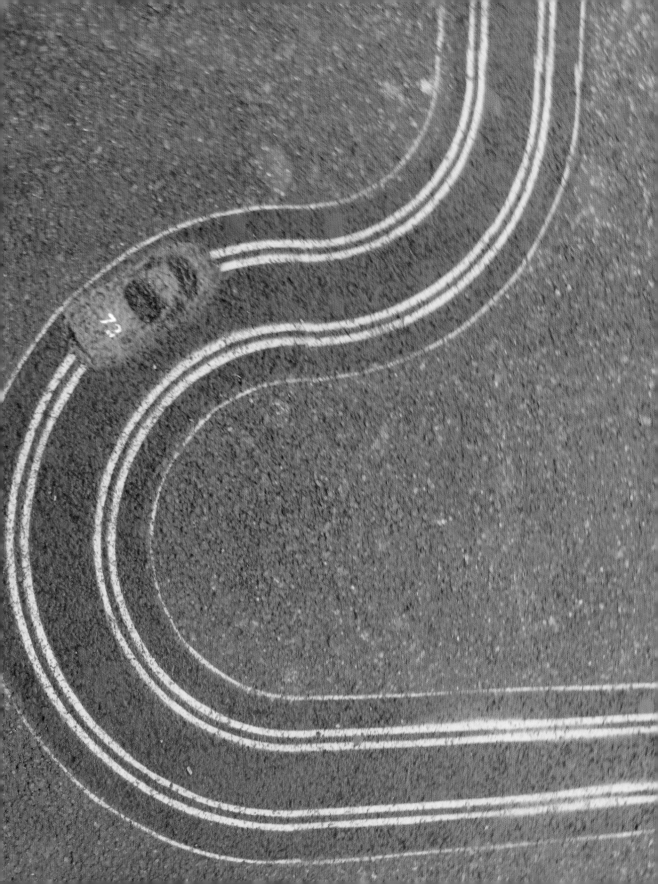

« START SOMETHING NEW EVERY DAY »

O for Office

When I first arrived in this office in February 2003, the space was empty. Since then, I have consciously filled it with things that "talk to me." I know the exact location of each object, each gadget—except when I come back from holiday: If someone has put something away, it becomes a problem, and I am lost. Visitors find the space chaotic. For me, it seems very organised.

P for
Paris

The first images that come to mind are from Jean-Luc Godard's *Breathless*. Jean-Paul Belmondo and Jean Seberg were, for me, the perfect incarnation of Parisian casual chic: fashionable without any particular fashion, something I especially like. I must admit I was somewhat disappointed when I visited Paris again. Men wore dull black or grey suits or jeans with leather jackets. Paris was a very exciting city in the 1970s, with its many little shops, tea salons and beautiful and simple cafés where you could stop in for a glass of wine and some charcuterie. I always believed that the French would like my clothes as long as I offered them a little fantasy. I was right, and our brand became quite successful in France, which is a big compliment for an Englishman. Clients were immediately taken by the touch of fantasy that is a mainstay of our collections: purple trim on a classic suit, a well-cut shirt of quality fabric with a big flower ... This type of detail liberated them, I believe, from an austerity that was not really theirs.

Our small shop on the rue de Grenelle is a tribute to the old-style cafés that have fascinated me since the 1970s. The shop used to sell coal and wine, and I kept almost all its original furnishings intact. It has a wonderful patina, enriched by all those who have come through its doors. This place is a manifesto against the uniformity that has been established by the giants of fashion. The biggest global brands, pressed by the banks who keep lending them more and more money, open stores every year that are identical.

P for .... Martin is a friend. We share a sense of observa-

tion that many think is strange. In fact, we are

both puzzled by other people's odd behaviour,

be it Saddam Hussein's suicidal attitude as he faced the American army, or the clothes British

people wear while on holiday. Martin's photographs capture the absurdity of certain moments,

caught in a mundane setting: for instance, an elegant woman at a fancy dinner with her finger

in her nose. His viewpoint is what has always

interested me.   Parr (Martin)

I met Pauline in 1967. I was tall
and skinny with long hair, and she was
gorgeous. That was, objectively, the most important moment of my life: The proof is that we are still
together. Pauline studied at the Royal College of Art in
London. At that time, they still taught dressmaking. She became
my teacher; she taught me everything I know about fashion: the
importance of the fabric, of its quality and drape; the way a garment
falls and is constructed and the importance of the slightest detail,
from the buttons to the hemline. I learned all the fundamental prin-
ciples of fashion from her.

P for

Pauline

I began taking photographs when I was eleven. My father was an amateur photographer who developed and printed his photographs in a darkroom he set up in our attic. Today, I shoot all our publicity campaigns as well as spreads for many fashion and design magazines. I find it a little frightening, but that's a good sign.

P for

Photography

P for
....

Politics

I have always been apolitical. Tony Blair once invited me to

10 Downing Street. Six or seven other people were present. In

the middle of the conversation, I said: "I don't know what you

are talking about." They all stared at me, but they didn't know

what they were talking about either.

P for

Post-It

I always have them next to me, day and night. I write down my thoughts, things I like, a sentence that caught my attention during a conversation. It can happen in the middle of a meeting, on a plane … I end up with a collection of phrases like: "Life is a puzzle." "As you get older, everything becomes clearer." "Everything falls into place, then you die." I have thousands of these. At the end of each week, I sort them and put them in see-through files. Nobody—absolutely nobody—can touch these. Later, I'll share them with my team and use them to add a touch of whimsy to a collection or to solve a problem.

I don't remember when this obsession with Post-its began, but I do remember that my father was always taking notes. He would grab a piece of paper to jot down a quote that he thought was interesting. I know that I am very much like my father, and I am proud of it. He was a good man.

Some t

(1) Start Some
(2) Take plea
(3) life work is not
hours or
it's about
(4) Look at th
the eyes of
admire and
(5) You can't do
(6) Make room
(7) Stop making
logic is pre
think differ

Start Something NEW
—
THE LOVE OF LIFE
—
NO ONE CARES HOW GOOD
YOU USED TO BE
— KEEP HUMBLE —

ALWAYS ASK WHAT
IS THE ALTERNATIVE

Remember to
do things
which are right
rather than things
that are easy

Seeing by doing.
Doing by seeing.

I DESCRIBE MY WORK AS SAVILE ROW MEETS MR. BEAN

P for
Price

Paul Smith clothes sell very well. They are not too expensive, but not inexpensive. Our collections are not elitist; clients buy them because they like what they see. This may sound naïve, but in today's fashion world, this is an unusual strategy. During our first twenty years, I could not afford to buy advertising pages in fashion magazines; my brand grew by word of mouth. Then as now, the company's financial condition has always been strong. I don't worry about profits or losses. I prefer to be free and relaxed, to enjoy every day of work. I know the production cost for every T-shirt, I know the profit the company will make from its sale, but I never think that we could have earned fifty more pounds. Furthermore, in fashion and elsewhere, consumers are knowledgeable and less naïve about pricing.

Queen

I have had the honour of meeting
Queen Elizabeth and other members of
the royal family on several occasions, but
November 24, 2000, the day I was knighted,
holds a very special place in my memory. Protocol
dictates that you cannot address the Queen until she
addresses you. After feeling the weight of the sword on my
shoulder, I sat quietly while other guests were awarded different honours or medals. I was getting restless, so I went
to chat with one of the staff of Buckingham Palace. He
explained to me that he was in a tight spot: It was his
girlfriend's birthday, and he had not bought her a
gift. I arranged for him to get a discount in our
store so he could buy her a gift fitting the occa-
sion. Visibly, my love for my work shows no
respite. Prince Andrew has come to visit
our workshop. My colleagues were
shocked when I called him "mate,"
but he was very relaxed about it.

R for Rabbits

In 1982, a friend told me that rabbits bring good luck. This is not true at all. To keep the joke going, I had a few made (in ceramic, porcelain and metal) and put them in our stores. These rabbits sold incredibly well, and we had to make more and more of them. I eventually had to slow down this "breeding" that threatened to take us over. Sometimes I think about unpopular animals, like snakes, spiders, rats or those that elicit fear or disgust. Their social position is quite unfair. Still, I don't particularly care for horses: They are too big; nature should have made them smaller.

S for

Sixties

Life in London at the age
of twenty was very exciting.
There was so much energy. We
felt that our generation was experi-
encing something that was completely
new. With very little money, you could live
in London and have fun. If you liked pink, you
would paint your entire apartment pink. Before The
Rolling Stones and The Beatles came on the scene, men
wore suits from age six to eighty. Then, everyone started
 dressing more casually in jeans and American T-shirts. Men
    started looking a little more feminine. Me too. When I met
        Pauline, I had long hair and looked like an Afghan hound.

S for

Smith (Patti)

I have been a fan of hers ever since I saw her in concert for the first time in 1972 (I saw The Doors perform in the same venue). I liked everything about her: her lifestyle, the fact that she wrote poetry and took photographs, that she was a painter and a rebel. I went to a concert she gave recently in Paris. I remember that I once gave her a pair of striped socks. The magic is still there. She is like a sister to me.

Probleme de taille 4/5cm a 300DPI

Souvenir

I don't have any souvenirs or memories from before the age of eleven. I never experienced a traumatic incident or a violent fight or a family drama. My sister is eight years older than I am, and my brother eleven, so they were never really around. At the age of eleven, I started spending time away from home and that was strange to me. When I was twelve, I realised that I was good at sports and that I was competitive.

They are the brand's most recognisable pattern. The thin bright stripes were wildly successful.

They were featured on shirts, polo shirts, hats and underwear … Of course the pattern has been

S for

Stripes

widely copied. We could have used a computer-generated process to make different size stripes

and colours, but I have insisted that each new series of stripes be drawn by hand. That adds a

tiny "human touch," a graceful imperfection that makes all the difference.

S for

Swimming

I started swimming in the 1980s. I was travelling extensively in those days, and, because I am quite tall, I often suffered from back pain. One day, I met an eighty-year-old man who was in superb shape and told me that he had been swimming every day for years and that it relaxed his body and his mind. Since then, I have tried to spend time in the water every day. I only swim for ten or fifteen minutes during the week, a little more on weekends. I like to stay fit. Swimming, even ten minutes each day, can be a wonderful antidote to work meetings and occasional tension. It wakes up the body, and I love the feeling of freedom—and the silence—you get in the water. It's a wonderful routine.

Taste (good and bad)

I am open to all kinds of taste. The only thing I cannot tolerate is bad manners.

I no longer think of things in terms of good or bad taste since the day I understood that those who are particularly disturbed by bad taste are usually the same people who have very bad taste.

I find it strange to want to be an arbiter of taste. Kitsch, for example, can be amusing. I like to mix what is considered to be in good taste with what is considered to be in bad taste. I like combining things that are shiny and matt, small and large, ultra-modern and old.

On the walls of my shops, a famous painting may hang next to a child's drawing. A signed photograph of Lucian Freud may be displayed next to a hand-decorated envelope sent by an anonymous person. For me, those juxtapositions represent a significant sense of order, where everything is in its place.

My strength, I believe, lies in the fact that I can sell as easily to an eighteen-year-old as I can to an eighty-year-old, to a student or to a very wealthy famous person; that's also my weak point, in that I am not always sufficiently focused. The elitist media prefer designers with a consistent and clear vision. If I tried to emulate them, it would not ring true, and I would not be myself. I would much rather be free and relaxed, and enjoy every day. I am not an anxious person.

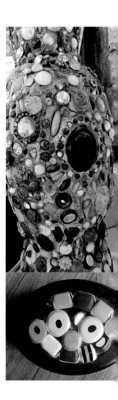

I do not use a computer. **T** for

And I don't have an e-mail

Technology

address. Only eight people

know my mobile number. I

don't send text messages. My wife, Pauline, does not have

a mobile phone. We take pleasure in writing letters to our

friends. I have nothing against new technology, but I don't

find it necessary to have so much information. When I see

adults become so dependent on these objects, I feel free,

child-like. I don't want my mind to be polluted with data

that doesn't interest me. The problem with today's means

of communication is that kids know what car their favour-

ite rock star drives, and that can make them feel bad about

their own situations, which then puts tremendous pressure

on them. If you can achieve a certain detachment, you can

enjoy a life free of worries, of comparisons, of thinking

that so and so is more famous or has more money than you

do. It's a philosophy for living.

I never thought about how I would grow my business;

it all happened gradually. Many of my collaborators design

on a computer; I prefer a piece of paper and a pencil. Many

have poked fun at me. They all know that I don't need a

computer to remember all that I've said. I never forget

anything. It's my way of earning the respect of the geeks.

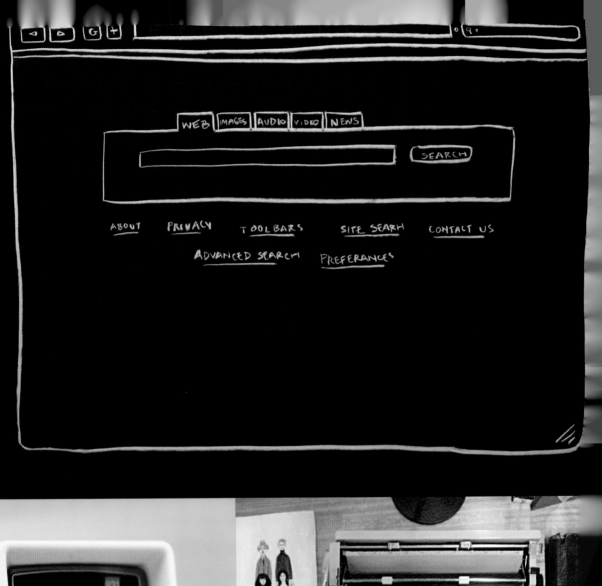

WEB | IMAGES | AUDIO | VIDEO | NEWS

SEARCH

ABOUT   PRIVACY   TOOLBARS   SITE SEARCH   CONTACT US
         ADVANCED SEARCH   PREFERANCES

« INSPIRATION IS ALL AROUND U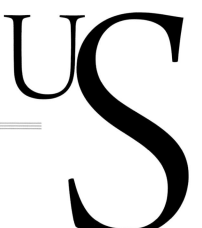S »

T for

Tokyo

I brought many electronic gadgets back from my first trips to Tokyo. Most of the robots in my collection came from the

amazing shops in Tokyo. The city's architecture, its energy and the hospitality of its people continue to attract me.

T for

I have travelled extensively
over the past fifteen years,
mainly for business. I fly once
or twice each week and never
complain about it. Sometimes,
I want to travel more. At one
point, I noticed that there was
a twenty-four-hour gap in my
schedule so I decided to go
and see the Great Wall of
China. I did it in one day and
night. I arranged a twenty-
four-hour trip to Beijing. To
plan your travel, you need to
be organised, choose your
objective and not need too
much sleep, which is the case
for me, as I typically sleep no
more than five hours. That's
what you might call light-
speed tourism. It gives you
a curious sensation—a little
surreal, but not unpleasant.
And when you return, you
feel really enriched.

Travel

U for Unbelievable

Amazing things happen to me . . . often, when I am riding my bicycle.

Recently, in Paris, I had some problems with the police. I decided to

photograph some police officers from behind, inside a tunnel. I made

the mistake of using a flash: They forced me to erase the photographs.

The very next day, I was stopped for using a mobile phone while riding

a bike, and the day after that, for having gone through a red light, still

on my bike . . .

V for

I received a bicycle on my eleventh birthday. Soon thereafter, I joined the local cycling club. My bicycle played a very important role in my childhood. I started racing at the age of twelve and quickly realised that I liked to compete. The older members of the club told me stories about Jacques Anquetil and Fausto Coppi.

We did not have a television and I remember having travelled many miles to buy a copy of *L'Équipe* from the only shop that sold it in our area. I also remember how I saved all my pocket money to buy the French newspaper. I wanted to become a professional racing cyclist, but when I was seventeen, I was hit by a car and had to give up my dream of participating in the Tour de France …

What I have kept from that time is my sense of competition and the meaning of the word "team." I spent three months in the hospital. With some of the other "long-term patients," I often went to a pub that was a hangout for students from a local art school. Talking to them, I discovered that there was a whole new world out there about which I knew nothing, and I thought, "Wow, that's exactly what I want to do!" Architecture, photography, design, graphics …

After that, I helped a friend open a clothing store, where I met Pauline, who, at the time, was already teaching in an art school … That's how I became who I am.

Vélo*

* Bicycle

W for
....

White Stripes

Everyone knows that Jack White, the leading member of this band, and the founder of multiple other bands, is an outstanding musician, one who can make music resonate like nobody else. But this guy is also very style-conscious. Notice how the colours red, white and black appear on all his album covers and in his music videos. Meg White, his female counterpart in The White Stripes, just married Patti Smith's son, Jackson. Those guys are perfect.

X for ....

The XX

Just as The White Stripes did, The xx understood the power of graphics and how it complemented their music.

Their manager happens to be the son of John Pawson, the architect and famous British personality.

You

I understood long ago that "you" are the most important person in my life. Not only do my clients pay my salary, but also the salaries of my entire team. I tell my colleagues over and over again that each person coming into one of our shops, whether a VIP, a student, a CEO, a celebrity or an anonymous person, young or old, whatever his or her story, each client is unique and important.

A B C D E F

H I J K L M

O P Q R S T

V W X Y O U

Z for

Zebra

Because they look

like horses wearing

pyjamas . . .

PHOTOGRAPHY CREDITS

All the photographs in this book were taken by Paul Smith except for the following:

Cover: ©Sandro Sodano

Getty Images—**p. 4**: ©Getty Images/Bill Heinsohn, **p. 18, top**: ©Getty Images/Bob Thomas, **lower right**: ©Getty Images/Bentley Archive/Popperfoto, **lower left**: ©Getty Images/AFP/Laurence Griffiths, **p. 19**: ©Getty Images/Popperfoto, **p. 27**: ©Getty Images/Hulton Archive/Terry O'Neill, **p. 29**: ©Getty Images/Redferns/Debi Doss, **p. 42**: ©Getty Images/Image Bank/Martin Poole, **p. 123**: ©Getty Images/Pictorial Parade, **p. 152, top**: ©Getty Images/Premium Archive/Denis O' Regan, **bottom**: ©Getty Images/Redferns/Dick Barnatt, **p. 165, top**: ©Getty Images/Iconica/Jeffrey Coolidge, **bottom left**: ©Getty Images/Iconica/Gregor Schuster.
Kharbine-Tapabor—**p. 28**: ©Kharbine-Tapabor/private collection HH.
AFP—**p. 101, bottom left**: ©AFP.
Gamma-Rapho—**p. 101, top and bottom right**: ©Keystone.
Paul Smith Collection—**pp. 6–7, p. 9** (photo Sang-Gon Kim), **p. 11** (top left: photo Sang-Gon Kim), **p. 13** (work by Bansky), **p. 14** (work by Phil Frost), **p. 23 and p. 25** (photos Sandro Sodano), **p. 26, p. 30** (photo Mariana Bassani), **p. 32, p. 33** (photo Sandro Sodano), **p. 50, p. 51** (work by Bansky), **p. 61, p. 80, p. 116** (photo Sandro Sodano), **p. 127** (photo Sandro Sodano), **p. 128, p. 130, p. 134, p. 144** (work by Ann Carrington), **p. 151, p. 161** (photo Daniel Bass), **p. 178, p. 179** (top), **p. 180, p. 181** (photo Sandro Sodano).
The White Stripes (album cover from "White Blood Cells"/Sympathy for the Record Industry)—**p. 282**.

ACKNOWLEDGMENTS

Olivier Wicker wishes to thank
Sophie Boilley and Alan Aboud
for their immeasurable help,
and Tiphaine Lévy-Frébault
for the translation.

The Stéphane Carrel film
Paul Smith: Gentleman Designer,
produced by Tabo Tabo and broadcast
on Arte, is available on DVD
(www.arteboutique.com).

Graphic Design: offparis.fr
Coordinating editor: Laure Lamendin
Proofreading: Philippe Rollet

English-language edition:

Editor: Laura Dozier
Designer: Shawn Dahl, dahlimama inc
Production Manager: Jules Thomson

Translated from the French by
Denise Raab Jacobs

Cataloging-in-Publication data has been
applied for and may be obtained from the
Library of Congress.

ISBN: 978-1-4197-0352-2

Printed and bound in China

10 9 8 7 6 5 4 3 2 1

Abrams books are available at special
discounts when purchased in quantity
for premiums and promotions as well
as fundraising or educational use.
Special editions can also be created
to specification. For details, contact
specialsales@abramsbooks.com
or the address below.

ABRAMS
THE ART OF BOOKS SINCE 1949

115 West 18th Street
New York, NY 10011
www.abramsbooks.com

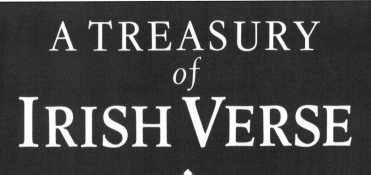

A TREASURY
of
IRISH VERSE

EDITED AND INTRODUCED BY DAVID GIBBON

~

DESIGNED BY PHILIP CLUCAS

~

Featuring the photography of Michael Diggin,
The Irish Tourist Board, Tony Ruta,
Philip Clucas and Colour Library Books

2937 A Treasury of Irish Verse
This edition published in 1997 by CLB
Distributed in the USA by BHB International, Inc.,
30 Edison Drive, Wayne, New Jersey 07470
©1992 CLB International
All rights reserved
Printed and bound in Singapore
ISBN 1-85833-702-X

A TREASURY
of
IRISH VERSE

The Dingle Peninsula, Co. Kerry

CLB

CONTENTS

Above: Glendalough Round
Tower, Co. Wicklow

INTRODUCTION

*P*oets write of many things. They write of love and passion, hope and despair, of the beauty of the things and places they love, and of the land they call home. They open their hearts, and in turn open our eyes, for they are themselves open to emotions that most of us are either not aware of or are unable to express. Although this is true of all people, of none is it truer than of the Irish. The songs they sing, and the poetry they write, is part of an extraordinarily rich heritage that stretches back into the dim, distant past, to the legends and myths with which Ireland is so richly endowed.

Great literary figures whose works are known the world over illuminate Ireland's literary history. But there are other, lesser known poets and writers whose work enriches that history in equal measure, from anonymous monks toiling in their tiny cells and poets whose names are almost forgotten, to those writers of today whose work has yet to achieve recognition.

Although this is not a book of poems and songs solely *about* Ireland, every page is *of* Ireland. The unique character of the Irish, their joy and their sadness, their hopes and aspirations, their deep and abiding love of their homeland, shines through in every line.

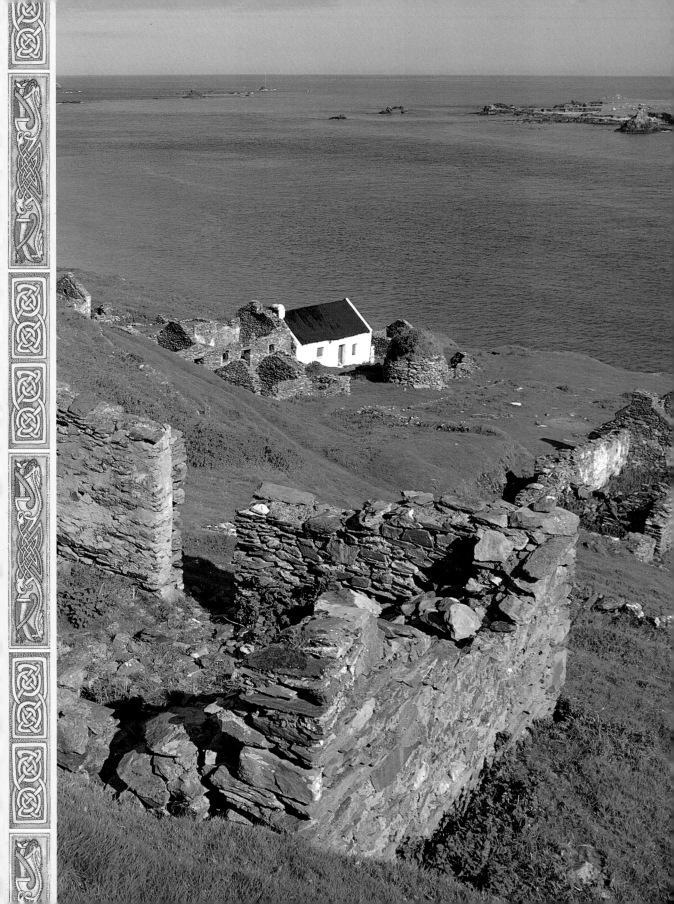

HOUSE ON A CLIFF

Indoors the tang of a tiny oil lamp. Outdoors
The winking signal on the waste of sea.
Indoors the sound of the wind. Outdoors the wind.
Indoors the locked heart and the lost key.

Outdoors the chill, the void, the siren. Indoors
The strong man pained to find his red blood cools,
While the blind clock grows louder, faster. Outdoors
The silent moon, the garrulous tides she rules.

Indoors ancestral curse-cum-blessing. Outdoors
The empty bowl of heaven, the empty deep.
Indoors a purposeful man who talks at cross
Purposes, to himself, in a broken sleep.

LOUIS MACNEICE (1907-1963)

Left: Clifftop house on
the Blasket Islands

IN CARROWDORE CHURCHYARD
AT THE GRAVE OF LOUIS MACNEICE

*Y*our ashes will not stir, even on this high ground,
However the wind tugs, the headstones shake.
This plot is consecrated, for your sake,
To what lies in the future tense. You lie
Past tension now, and spring is coming round
Igniting flowers on the peninsula.

Your ashes will not fly, however the rough winds burst
Through the wild brambles and the reticent trees.
All we may ask of you we have. The rest
Is not for publication, will not be heard.
Maguire, I believe, suggested a blackbird
And over your grave a phrase from Euripides.

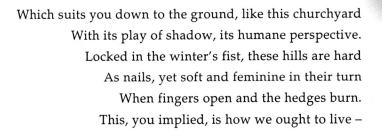

Which suits you down to the ground, like this churchyard
With its play of shadow, its humane perspective.
Locked in the winter's fist, these hills are hard
As nails, yet soft and feminine in their turn
When fingers open and the hedges burn.
This, you implied, is how we ought to live –

The ironical, loving crush of roses against snow,
Each fragile, solving ambiguity. So
From the pneumonia of the ditch, from the ague
Of the blind poet and the bombed-out town you bring
The all-clear to the empty holes of spring;
Rinsing the choked mud, keeping the colours new.

DEREK MAHON (1941-)

14

JUNE

*B*room out the floor now, lay the fender by,
And plant this bee-sucked bough of woodbine there,
    And let the window down. The butterfly
Floats in upon the sunbeam, and the fair
    Tanned face of June, the nomad gipsy, laughs
Above her widespread wares, the while she tells
    The farmers' fortunes in the fields, and quaffs
The water from the spider-peopled wells.

    The hedges all are drowned in green grass seas,
And bobbing poppies flare like Elmo's light,
    While siren-like the pollen stainéd bees
Drone in the clover depths. And up the height
    The cuckoo's voice is hoarse and broke with joy.
And on the lowland crops the crows make raid,
    Nor fear the clappers of the farmer's boy,
Who sleeps, like drunken Noah, in the shade.

    And loop this red rose in that hazel ring
    That snares your little ear, for June is short
    And we must joy in it and dance and sing,
        And from her bounty draw her rosy worth.
        Ay! soon the swallows will be flying south,
        The wind wheel north to gather in the snow,
        Even the roses spilt on youth's red mouth
        Will soon blow down the road all roses go.

FRANCIS LEDWIDGE (1891-1917)

THE FORGE

All I know is a door into the dark.
Outside, old axles and iron hoops rusting;
Inside, the hammered anvil's short-pitched ring,
The unpredictable fantail of sparks
Or hiss when a new shoe toughens in water.
The anvil must be somewhere in the centre,
Horned as a unicorn, at one end square,
Set there immovable: an altar
Where he expends himself in shape and music.
Sometimes, leather-aproned, hairs in his nose,
He leans out on the jamb, recalls a clatter
Of hoofs where traffic is flashing in rows;
Then grunts and goes in, with a slam and flick
To beat real iron out, to work the bellows.

SEAMUS HEANEY (1939-)

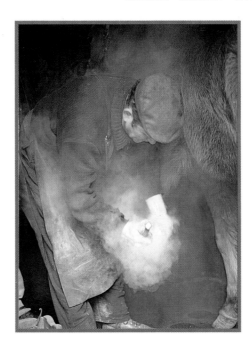

DARK ROSALEEN

(From the Irish of Costello)

O my Dark Rosaleen,
    Do not sigh, do not weep!
The priests are on the ocean green,
    They march along the Deep.
There's wine ... from the royal Pope
    Upon the ocean green;
And Spanish ale shall give you hope,
    My Dark Rosaleen!
    My own Rosaleen!
Shall glad your heart, shall give you hope,
Shall give you health, and help, and hope,
    My Dark Rosaleen.

Over hills and through dales,
    Have I roamed for your sake;
All yesterday I sailed with sails
    On river and on lake.
The Erne ... at its highest flood
    I dashed across unseen,
For there was lightning in my blood,
    My Dark Rosaleen!
    My own Rosaleen!
Oh! there was lightning in my blood,
Red lightning lightened through my blood,
    My Dark Rosaleen!

All day long in unrest
    To and fro do I move,
The very soul within my breast
    Is wasted for you, love!

continued...

The heart ... in my bosom faints
　　　　To think of you my Queen,
My life of life, my saint of saints,
　　　　My Dark Rosaleen!
　　　　My own Rosaleen!
To hear your sweet and sad complaints,
My life, my love, my saint of saints,
　　　　My Dark Rosaleen!

Woe and pain, pain and woe,
　　　　Are my lot night and noon,
To see your bright face clouded so,
　　　　Like to the mournful moon.
But yet ... I will rear your throne
　　　　Again in golden sheen;
'Tis you shall reign, shall reign alone,
　　　　My Dark Rosaleen!
　　　　My own Rosaleen!
'Tis you shall have the golden throne,
'Tis you shall reign, and reign alone
　　　　My Dark Rosaleen!

Over dews, over sands
　　　　Will I fly for your weal;
Your holy delicate white hands
　　　　Shall girdle me with steel.
At home ... in your emerald bowers,
　　　　From morning's dawn till e'en,
You'll pray for me, my flower of flowers,
　　　　My Dark Rosaleen!
　　　　My fond Rosaleen!
You'll think of me through daylight's hours,
My virgin flower, my flower of flowers,
　　　　My Dark Rosaleen!　　　　　continued...

Inisheer, easternmost of the Aran Islands

I could scale the blue air,
 I could plough the high hills,
Oh, I could kneel all night in prayer,
 To heal your many ills!
And one … beamy smile from you
 Would float like light between
My toils and me, my own, my true,
 My Dark Rosaleen!
 My fond Rosaleen!
Would give me life and soul anew,
A second life, a soul anew,
 My Dark Rosaleen!

O! the Erne shall run red
 With redundance of blood,
The earth shall rock beneath our tread,
 And flames wrap hill and wood,
And gun-peal, and slogan cry,
 Wake many a glen serene,
Ere you shall fade, ere you shall die,
 My Dark Rosaleen!
 My own Rosaleen!
The Judgement Hour must first be nigh,
Ere you can fade, ere you can die,
 My Dark Rosaleen!

JAMES CLARENCE MANGAN (1803-1849)

Left: Macgillycuddy's
Reeks, Co. Kerry

The Ring of Kerry

HE WISHES FOR THE CLOTHS OF HEAVEN

*H*ad I the heavens' embroidered cloths,
Enwrought with golden and silver light,
  The blue and the dim and the dark cloths
Of night and light and the half-light,
  I would spread the cloths under your feet:
But I, being poor, have only my dreams;
  I have spread my dreams under your feet;
Tread softly because you tread on my dreams.

W.B. YEATS (1865-1939)

GOING HOME TO MAYO, WINTER, 1949

Leaving behind us the alien, foreign city of Dublin
My father drove through the night in an old Ford Anglia,
His five-year-old son in the seat beside him,
The rexine seat of red leatherette,
And a yellow moon peeped in through the windscreen.
'Daddy, Daddy,' I cried, 'Pass out the moon,'
But no matter how hard he drove he could not pass out the moon.
Each town we passed through was another milestone
And their names were magic passwords into eternity:
Kilcock, Kinnegad, Strokestown, Elphin,
Tarmonbarry, Tulsk, Ballaghderreen, Ballavarry;
Now we were in Mayo and the next stop was Turlough,
The village of Turlough in the heartland of Mayo,
And my father's mother's house, all oil-lamps and women,
And my bedroom over the public bar below,
And in the morning cattle-cries and cock-crows:
Life's seemingly seamless garment gorgeously rent
By their screeches and bellowings. And in the evenings
I walked with my father in the high grass down by the river
Talking with him – an unheard-of thing in the city.

But home was not home and the moon could be no more outflanked
Than the daylight nightmare of Dublin city:
Back down along the canal we chugged into the city
And each lock-gate tolled our mutual doom;
And railing and palings and asphalt and traffic-lights,
And blocks after blocks of so-called 'new' tenements –
Thousands of crosses of loneliness planted
In the narrowing grave of the life of the father;
In the wide, wide cemetery of the boy's childhood.

PAUL DURCAN (1944-)

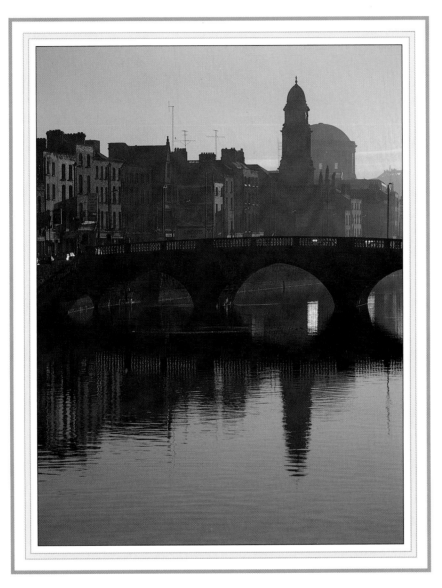

The River Liffey, Dublin City

IRELAND

I called you by sweet names by wood and linn,
You answered not because my voice was new,
And you were listening for the hounds of Finn
    And the long hosts of Lugh.

And so, I came unto a windy height
And cried my sorrow, but you heard no wind,
For you were listening to small ships in flight,
    And the wail on hills behind.

And then I left you, wandering the war
Armed with will, from distant goal to goal,
To find you at the last free as of yore,
    Or die to save your soul.

And then you called to us from far and near
To bring your crown from out the deeps of time,
It is my grief your voice I couldn't hear
    In such a distant clime.

FRANCIS LEDWIDGE (1891-1917)

Left: The Poulnabrone dolmen, Co. Clare

THE LAKE ISLE OF INNISFREE

I will arise and go now, and go to Innisfree,
And a small cabin build there, of clay and wattles made:
Nine bean-rows will I have there, a hive for the honey-bee,
And live alone in the bee-loud glade.

And I shall have some peace there, for peace comes dropping slow,
Dropping from the veils of the morning to where the cricket sings;
There midnight's all a glimmer, and noon a purple glow,
And evening full of the linnet's wings.

I will arise and go now, for always night and day
I hear lake water lapping with low sounds by the shore;
While I stand on the roadway, or on the pavements grey,
I hear it in the deep heart's core.

W.B. YEATS (1865-1939)

AT A POTATO DIGGING

A mechanical digger wrecks the drill,
Spins up a dark shower of roots and mould.
Labourers swarm in behind, stoop to fill
Wicker creels. Fingers go dead in the cold.

Like crows attacking crow-black fields, they stretch
A higgledy line from hedge to headland;
Some pairs keep breaking ragged ranks to fetch
A full creel to the pit and straighten, stand

Tall for a moment but soon stumble back
To fish a new load from the crumbled surf.
Heads bow, trunks bend, hands fumble towards the black
Mother. Processional stooping through the turf

Recurs mindlessly as autumn. Centuries
Of fear and homage to the famine god
Toughen the muscles behind their humbled knees,
Make a seasonal altar of the sod.

SEAMUS HEANEY (1939-)

OPENING LINES FROM
THE MIDNIGHT COURT

By the brink of the river I'd often walk,
    on a meadow fresh, in the heavy dew,
along the woods, in the mountain's heart,
    happy and brisk in the brightening dawn.

My heart would lighten to see Loch Gréine,
    the land, the view, the sky horizon,
the sweet and delightful set of the mountains
    looming their heads up over each other.

It would brighten a heart worn out with time,
    or spent, or faint, or filled with pain
– or the withered, the sour, without wealth or means –
    to gaze for a while across the woods
at the shoals of ducks on the cloudless bay
    and a swan between them, sailing with them,
at fishes jumping on high for joy,
    the flash of a stripe-bellied glittering perch,
the hue of the lake, the blue of the waves
    heavy and strong as they rumble in.

There were birds in the trees, cintent and gay,
    a leaping doe in the wood nearby,
sounding horns, a crowd in view,
    and Reynard ahead of the galloping hounds.

BRIAN MERRIMAN (1749-1805)

Right: Lough Acumeen, Co. Kerry

OCTOBER

O leafy yellowness you create for me
A world that was and now is poised above time,
    I do not need to puzzle out Eternity
As I walk this arboreal street on the edge of a town.
The breeze too, even the temperature
And pattern of movement is precisely the same
    As broke my heart for youth passing. Now I am sure
    Of something. Something will be mine wherever I am.
I want to throw myself on the public street without caring
For anything but the prayering that the earth offers.
    It is October all over my life and the light is staring
    As it caught me once in a plantation by the fox coverts.
A man is ploughing ground for winter wheat
And my nineteen years weigh heavily on my feet.

PATRICK KAVANAGH (1904-1967)

HER VOICE COULD
NOT BE SOFTER

*S*uddenly in the dark wood·
She turned from my arms and cried
As if her soul were lost,
And O too late I knew,
Although the blame was mine,
Her voice could not be softer
When she told it in confession.

AUSTIN CLARKE (1896-1974)

AN OLD WOMAN OF THE ROADS

O, to have a little house!
  To own the hearth and stool and all!
    The heaped up sods against the fire,
      The pile of turf against the wall!

  To have a clock with weights and chains
    And pendulum swinging up and down!
      A dresser filled with shining delph,
        Speckled and white and blue and brown!

I could be busy all the day
  Clearing and sweeping hearth and floor,
    And fixing on their shelf again
      My white and blue and speckled store!

  I could be quiet there at night
    Beside the fire and by myself,
      Sure of a bed and loth to leave
        The ticking clock and the shining delph!

Och! but I'm weary of mist and dark,
  And roads where there's never a house nor bush,
    And tired I am of bog and road,
      And the crying wind and the lonesome hush!

  And I am praying to God on high,
    And I am praying Him night and day,
      For a little house – a house of my own –
        Out of the wind's and the rain's way.

PADRAIC COLUM (1881-1972)

THE SUNLIGHT ON
THE GARDEN

The sunlight on the garden
Hardens and grows cold,
We cannot cage the minute
Within its nets of gold,
When all is told
We cannot beg for pardon.

Our freedom as free lances
Advances towards its end;
The earth compels, upon it
Sonnets and birds descend;
And soon, my friend,
We shall have no time for dances.

The sky was good for flying
Defying the church bells
And every evil iron
Siren and what it tells:
The earth compels,
We are dying, Egypt, dying

And not expecting pardon,
Hardened in heart anew,
But glad to have sat under
Thunder and rain with you,
And grateful too
For sunlight on the garden.

LOUIS MACNEICE (1907-1963)

THE LIMERICK TRAIN

*H*urtling between hedges now, I see
Green desolation stretch on either hand
While sunlight blesses all magnanimously.

The gods and heroes are gone for good and
Men evacuate each Munster valley
And midland plain, gravelly Connaught land

And Leinster town. Who, I wonder, fully
Understands the imminent predicament,
Sprung from rooted suffering and folly?

Broken castles tower, lost order's monument,
Splendour crumbling in sun and rain,
Witnesses to all we've squandered and spent,

But no Phoenix rises from that ruin
Although the wild furze in yellow pride
Explodes in bloom above each weed and stone,

Promise ablaze on every mountainside
After the centuries' game of pitch-and-toss
Separates what must live from what has died.

A church whips past, proclaiming heavy loss
Amounting to some forty thousand pounds;
A marble Christ unpaid for on His Cross

Accepts the Limerick train's irreverent sound,
Relinquishes great power to little men –
A river flowing still, but underground.

Wheels clip the quiet counties. Now and then
I see a field where like an effigy
In rushy earth, there stands a man alone

Carrigogunnel Castle, Co. Limerick

continued…

Lifting his hand in salutation. He
Disappears almost as soon as he is seen,
Drowned in distant anonymity.

We have travelled far, the journey has been
Costly, tormented odyssey through night;
And now, noting the unmistakable green,

The pools and trees that spring into the sight,
The sheep that scatter madly, wheel and run,
Quickly transformed to terrified leaping white,

I think of what the land has undergone
And find the luminous events of history
Intolerable as staring at the sun.

Only twenty miles to go and I'll be
Home. Seeing two crows low over the land,
I recognize the land's uncertainty,

The unsensational surrender and
Genuflexion to the busy stranger
Whose power in pocket brings him power in hand.

Realizing now how dead is anger
Such as sustained us at the very start
With possibility in time of danger,

I know why we have turned away, apart
(I'm moving still but so much time has sped)
From the dark realities of the heart.

From my window now, I try to look ahead
And know, remembering what's been done and said
That we must always cherish, and reject, the dead.

BRENDAN KENNELLY (1936-)

'THE APPLES RIPEN UNDER YELLOWING LEAVES'

The apples ripen under yellowing leaves,
    And in the farm yards by the little bay
The shadows come and go amid the sheaves,
    And on the long dry inland winding way:
Where, in the thinning boughs each air bereaves
Faint sunlights golden, and the spider weaves.
Grey are the low-laid sleepy hills, and grey
    The autumn solitude of the sea day,
Where from the deep 'mid-channel, less and less
    You hear along the pale east afternoon
A sound, uncertain as the silence, swoon –
The tide's sad voice ebbing toward loneliness:
And past the sands and seas' blue level line,
Ceaseless, the faint far murmur of the brine.

THOMAS CAULFIELD IRWIN (1823-1892)

Right: Connemara, Co. Galway

MARTHA BLAKE

*B*efore the day is everywhere
    And the timid warmth of sleep
Is delicate on limb, she dares
    The silence of the street
Until the double bells are thrown back
    For Mass and echoes bound
In the chapel yard, O then her soul
    Makes bold in the arms of sound.

But in the shadow of the nave
    Her well-taught knees are humble,
She does not see through any saint
    That stands in the sun
With veins of lead, with painful crown:
    She waits that dreaded coming,
When all the congregation bows
    And none may look up.

The word is said, the Word sent down,
    The miracle is done
Beneath those hands that have been rounded
    Over the embodied cup,
And with a few, she leaves her place
    Kept by an east-filled window
And kneels at the communion rail
    Starching beneath her chin.

She trembles for the Son of Man,
    While the priest is murmuring
What she can scarcely tell, her heart
    Is making such a stir;
But when he picks a particle
    And she puts out her tongue,
That joy is the glittering of candles
    And benediction sung.

Her soul is lying in the Presence
    Until her senses, one
By one, desiring to attend her,
    Come as for feast and run
So fast to share the sacrament,
    Her mouth must mother them:
'Sweet tooth grow wise, lip, gum be gentle,
    I touch a purple hem.'

Afflicted by that love she turns
    To multiply her praise,
Goes over all the foolish words
    And finds they are the same;
But now she feels within her breast
    Such calm that she is silent,
For soul can never bè immodest
    Where body may not listen.

continued…

On a holy day of obligation
    I saw her first in prayer,
But mortal eye had been too late
    For all that thought could dare.
The flame in heart is never grieved
    That pride and intellect
Were cast below, when God revealed
    A heaven for this earth.

So to begin the common day
    She needs a miracle,
Knowing the safety of angels
    That see her home again,
Yet ignorant of all the rest,
    The hidden grace that people
Hurrying to business
    Look after in the street.

AUSTIN CLARKE (1896-1974)

ACHILL

im chaonai uaigneach nach mór go bhfeicim an lá

I lie and imagine a first light gleam in the bay
   After one more night of erosion and nearer the grave,
Then stand and gaze from a window at break of day
   As a shearwater skims the ridge of an incoming wave;
And I think of my son a dolphin in the Aegean,
   A sprite among sails knife-bright in a seasonal wind,
And wish he were here where currachs walk on the ocean
   To ease with his talk the solitude locked in my mind.

I sit on a stone after lunch and consider the glow
   Of the sun through mist, a pearl bulb containèdly fierce;
A rain-shower darkens the schist for a minute or so
   Then it drifts away and the sloe-black patches disperse.
Croagh Patrick towers like Naxos over the water
   And I think of my daughter at work on her difficult art
And wish she were with me now between thrush and plover,
   Wild thyme and sea-thrift, to lift the weight from my heart.

The young sit smoking and laughing on the bridge at evening
   Like birds on a telephone pole or notes on a score.
A tin whistle squeals in the parlour, once more it is raining,
   Turfsmoke inclines and a wind whines under the door;
And I lie and imagine the lights going on in the harbour
   Of white-housed Náousa, your clear definition at night,
And wish you were here to upstage my disconsolate labour
   As I glance through a few thin pages and switch off the light.

DEREK MAHON (1941-)

Left: Achill Island, Co. Mayo

THE LAPFUL OF NUTS

*W*hene'er I see soft hazel eyes
    And nut-brown curls,
I think of those bright days I spent
    Among the Limerick girls;
When up through Cratla woods I went,
    Nutting with thee;
And we pluck'd the glossy clustering fruit
    From many a bending tree.

    Beneath the hazel boughs we sat,
        Thou, love, and I,
    And the gather'd nuts lay in thy lap,
        Beneath thy downcast eye:
    But little we thought of the store we'd won,
        I, love, or thou;
    For our hearts were full, and we dare not own
        The love that's spoken now.

Oh there's wars for willing hearts in Spain,
    And high Germanie!
And I'll come back, ere long again,
    With knightly fame and fee:
And I'll come back, if I ever come back,
    Faithful to thee,
That sat with thy white lap full of nuts
    Beneath the hazel tree.

SAMUEL FERGUSON (1810-1886)

THE ROCK OF CASHEL

*R*oyal and Saintly Cashel! I would gaze
    Upon the wreck of thy departed powers,
    Not in the dewy light of matin hours,
Nor the meridian pomp of summer's blaze,
But at the close of dim autumnal days,
    When the sun's parting glance, through slanting showers
    Sheds o'er thy rock-throned battlements and towers
Such awful gleams as brighten o'er Decay's
Prophetic cheek. At such a time, methinks,
    There breathes from thy lone courts and voiceless aisles
A melancholy moral, such as sinks
    On the lone traveller's heart, amid the piles
Of vast Persepolis on her mountain stand,
Or Thebes half buried in the desert sand.

SIR AUBREY DE VERE (1788-1846)

Right: The Rock of Cashel

THE AVENUE

*N*ow that we've come to the end
I've been trying to piece it together,
Not that distance makes anything clearer.
It began in the half-light
While we walked through the dawn chorus
After a party that lasted all night,
With the blackbird, the wood-pigeon,
The song-thrush taking a bludgeon
To a snail, our taking each other's hand
As if the whole world lay before us.

PAUL MULDOON (1951-)

Lough Dan, Co. Wicklow

The Conner Pass, Co. Kerry

AFTER THE IRISH OF
EGAN O'RAHILLY

*W*ithout flocks or cattle or the curved horns
Of cattle, in a drenching night without sleep,
My five wits on the famous uproar
Of the wave toss like ships,
And I cry for boyhood, long before
Winkle and dogfish had defiled my lips.

O if he lived, the prince who sheltered me,
And his company who gave me entry
On the river of the Laune,
Whose royalty stood sentry
Over intricate harbours, I and my own
Would not be desolate in Dermot's country.

Fierce McCarthy Mor whose friends were welcome.
McCarthy of the Lee, a slave of late,
McCarthy of Kanturk whose blood
Has dried underfoot:
Of all my princes not a single word –
Irrevocable silence ails my heart,

My heart shrinks in me, my heart ails
That every hawk and royal hawk is lost;
From Cashel to the far sea
Their birthright is dispersed
Far and near, night and day, by robbery
And ransack, every town oppressed.

continued…

Right: The Twelve Bens, Connemara

Take warning wave, take warning crown of the sea,
I, O'Rahilly – witless from your discords –
Were Spanish sails again afloat
And rescue on your tides,
Would force this outcry down your wild throat,
Would make you swallow these Atlantic words.

EAVAN BOLAND (1945-)

Aran Islands, Co. Galway

IN THE SEVEN WOODS

I have heard the pigeons of the Seven Woods
Make their faint thunder, and the garden bees
   Hum in the lime-tree flowers; and put away
The unavailing outcries and the old bitterness
   That empty the heart. I have forgot awhile
Tara uprooted, and new commonness
   Upon the throne and crying about the streets
And hanging its paper flowers from post to post,
   Because it is alone of all things happy.
I am contented, for I know that Quiet
   Wanders laughing and eating her wild heart
Among pigeons and bees, while that Great Archer,
   Who but awaits His hour to shoot, and still hangs
A cloudy quiver over Pairc-na-lee.

W.B. YEATS (1865-1939)

SHE MOVED THROUGH THE FAIR

My young love said to me, 'My brothers won't mind,
And my parents won't slight you for your lack of kind.'
    Then she stepped away from me, and this she did say,
'It will not be long, love, till our wedding day.'

    She stepped away from me and she moved through the fair,
And fondly I watched her go here and go there,
    Then she went her way homeward with one star awake,
As the swan in the evening moves over the lake.

    The people were saying no two were e'er wed
But one had a sorrow that never was said,
    And I smiled as she passed with her goods and her gear,
And that was the last that I saw of my dear.

    I dreamt it last night that my young love came in,
So softly she entered, her feet made no din;
    She came close beside me, and this she did say,
'It will not be long, love, till our wedding day.'

PADRAIC COLUM (1881-1972)

71
~

SEPTEMBER 1913

What need you, being come to sense,
But fumble in a greasy till
And add the halfpence to the pence
And prayer to shivering prayer, until
You have dried the marrow from the bone?
For men were born to pray and save:
Romantic Ireland's dead and gone,
It's with O'Leary in the grave.

Yet they were of a different kind,
The names that stilled your childish play,
They have gone about the world like wind,
But little time had they to pray
For whom the hangman's rope was spun,
And what, God help us, could they save?
Romantic Ireland's dead and gone,
It's with O'Leary in the grave.

Was it for this the wild geese spread
The grey wing upon every tide;
For this that all that blood was shed,
For this Edward Fitzgerald died,
And Robert Emmet and Wolfe Tone,
All that delirium of the brave?
Romantic Ireland's dead and gone,
It's with O'Leary in the grave.

Yet could we turn the years again,
And call those exiles as they were
In all their loneliness and pain,
You'd cry, 'Some woman's yellow hair
Has maddened every mother's son':
They weighed so lightly what they gave.
But let them be, they're dead and gone,
They're with O'Leary in the grave.

St Maolcheador's,
Kilmalkedar,
Dingle Peninsula

W.B. YEATS (1865-1939)

REST ONLY IN THE GRAVE

I rode till I reached the House of Wealth—
'Twas filled with riot and blighted health.

I rode till I reached the House of Love—
'Twas vocal with sighs beneath and above!

I rode till I reached the House of Sin—
There were shrieks and curses without and within.

I rode till I reached the House of Toil—
Its inmates had nothing to bake or boil.

I rode in search of the House of Content
But never could reach it, far as I went!

The House of Quiet, for strong and weak
And poor and rich, I have still to seek—

That House is narrow, and dark, and small—
But the only Peaceful House of all.

JAMES CLARENCE MANGAN (1803-1849)

THE DAWNING OF THE DAY

At early dawn I once had been
　　Where Lene's blue waters flow,
When summer bid the groves be green,
　　The lamp of light to glow.
As on by bower, and town, and tower,
　　And widespread fields I stray,
I meet a maid in the greenwood shade
　　At the dawning of the day.

　　Her feet and beauteous head were bare,
　　　　No mantle fair she wore;
　　But down her waist fell golden hair,
　　　　That swept the tall grass o'er.
　　With milking-pail she sought the vale,
　　　　And bright her charms' display;
　　Outshining far the morning star
　　　　At the dawning of the day.

　　Beside me sat that maid divine
　　　Where grassy banks outspread.
　'Oh, let me call thee ever mine,
　　Dear maid,' I sportive said.
'False man, for shame, why bring me blame?'
　　She cried, and burst away –
The sun's first light pursued her flight
　　At the dawning of the day.

EDWARD WALSH (1805-1851)

Right: Schull, Co. Cork

76
~

THE DESERTER'S MEDITATION

*I*f sadly thinking, with spirits sinking,
　　Could more than drinking my cares compose,
A cure for sorrow from sighs I'd borrow,
　　And hope to-morrow would end my woes.
But as in wailing there's nought availing,
　　And Death unfailing will strike the blow,
Then for that reason, and for a season,
　　Let us be merry before we go.

To joy a stranger, a way-worn ranger,
　　In every danger my course I've run;
Now hope all ending, and death befriending
　　His last aid lending, my cares are done.
No more a rover, or hapless lover,
　　My griefs are over – my glass runs low;
Then for that reason, and for a season,
　　Let us be merry before we go.

JOHN PHILPOT CURRAN (1750-1817)

THE MEMORY OF THE DEAD

Who fears to speak of Ninety-Eight?
    Who blushes at the name?
When cowards mock the patriot's fate
    Who hangs his head for shame?
He's all a knave or half a slave
    Who slights his country thus:
But a true man, like you, man,
    Will fill your glass with us.

We drink the memory of the brave,
    The faithful and the few –
Some lie far off beyond the wave,
    Some sleep in Ireland, too;
All, all are gone – but still lives on
    The fame of those who died;
And true men, like you, men
    Remember them with pride.

Some on the shores of distant lands
    Their weary hearts have laid,
And by the stranger's heedless hands
    Their lonely graves were made;
But though their clay be far away
    Beyond the Atlantic foam,
In true men, like you, men
    Their spirit's still at home.

The dust of some is Irish earth;
    Among their own they rest;
And the same land that gave them birth
    Has caught them to her breast;
And we will pray that from their clay
    Full many a race may start
Of true men, like you, men,
    To act as brave a part.

They rose in dark and evil days
    To right their native land;
They kindled here a living blaze
    That nothing shall withstand.
Alas! that Might can vanquish Right –
    They fell, and passed away;
But true men, like you, men,
    Are plenty here today.

Then here's their memory – may it be
    For us a guiding light,
To cheer our strife for liberty,
    And teach us to unite!
Through good and ill, be Ireland's still,
    Though sad as theirs, your fate;
And true men, be you, men,
    Like those of Ninety-Eight.

JOHN KELLS INGRAM (1823-1907)

Left: Kilmainham Gaol, Dublin

The statue of a horseman within the
ruins of a church at Annagh, Tralee

A VISION OF CONNAUGHT
IN THE THIRTEENTH CENTURY

I walked entranced
  Through a land of Morn;
The sun, with wondrous excess of light,
  Shone down and glanced
    Over seas of corn
And lustrous gardens aleft and right.
  Even in the clime
    Of resplendent Spain,
Beams no such sun upon such a land;
  But it was the time,
    'Twas in the reign,
Of Cáhal Mór of the Wine-red Hand.

  Anon stood nigh
    By my side a man
Of princely aspect and port sublime.
  Him queried I –
    'O, my Lord and Khan,
What clime is this, and what golden time?'
  When he – 'The clime
    Is a clime to praise,
The clime is Erin's, the green and bland;
  And it is the time,
    These be the days,
Of Cáhal Mór of the Wine-red Hand!'

  Then I saw the thrones,
    And circling fires,
And a Dome rose near me, as by a spell,
  Whence flowed the tones
    Of silver lyres,
And many voices in wreathéd swell;
  And their thrilling chime
    Fell on mine ears
As the heavenly hymn of an angel-band –
  'It is now the time,
    These be the years,
Of Cáhal Mór of the Wine-red Hand!'

  I sought the hall,
    And, behold! – a change
From light to darkness, from joy to woe!
  King, nobles, all,
    Looked aghast and strange;
The minstrel-group sate in dumbest show!
  Had some great crime
    Wrought this dread amaze,
This terror? None seemed to understand
  'Twas then the time,
    We were in the days,
Of Cáhal Mór of the Wine-red Hand.

continued…

I again walked forth;
        But lo! the sky
Showed fleckt with blood, and an alien sun
        Glared from the north
        And there stood on high,
Amid his shorn beams, a skeleton!
        It was by the stream
        Of the castled Maine,
One Autumn eve, in the Teuton's land,
        That I dreamed this dream
        Of the time and reign
Of Cáhal Mór of the Wine-red Hand!

JAMES CLARENCE MANGAN (1803-1849)

The tomb of Strongbow in Christ
Church Cathedral, Dublin

THE BELLS OF SHANDON

*W*ith deep affection and recollection
 I often think of the Shandon bells,
Whose sounds so wild would, in days of childhood,
 Fling round my cradle their magic spells.
On this I ponder, where'er I wander
 And thus grow fonder, sweet Cork, of thee;
  With thy bells of Shandon,
  That sound so grand on
 The pleasant waters of the river Lee.

I have heard bells chiming full many a clime in,
 Tolling sublime in cathedral shrine;
While at a glib rate brass tongues would vibrate,
 But all their music spoke nought to thine;
For memory dwelling on each proud swelling
 Of thy belfry knelling its bold notes free,
  Made the bells of Shandon
  Sound far more grand on
 The pleasant waters of the river Lee.

The church of
St Anne's, Shandon,
Cork City

The River Lee, Cork City

I have heard bells tolling 'old Adrian's mole' in,
  Their thunder rolling from the Vatican,
With cymbals glorious, swinging uproarious
  In the gorgeous turrets of Notre Dame;
    But thy sounds were sweeter than the dome of Peter
    Flings o'er the Tiber, pealing solemnly.
        Oh! the bells of Shandon
        Sound far more grand on
    The pleasant waters of the river Lee.

    There's a bell in Moscow, while on tower and kiosko
    In St Sophia the Turkman gets,
And loud in air calls men to prayer
    From the tapering summit of tall minarets.
Such empty phantom I freely grant 'em,
    But there's an anthem more dear to me:
        'Tis the bells of Shandon,
        That sound so grand on
    The pleasant waters of the river Lee.

FRANCIS SYLVESTER MAHONY (1804-1866)

87
~

SNOW

The room was suddenly rich and the great bay-window was
 Spawning snow and pink roses against it
 Soundlessly collateral and incompatible:
 World is suddener than we fancy it.

 World is crazier and more of it than we think,
 Incorrigibly plural. I peel and portion
 A tangerine and spit the pips and feel
 The drunkenness of things being various.

 And the fire flames with a bubbling sound for world
 Is more spiteful and gay than one supposes –
 On the tongue on the eyes on the ears in the palms of one's hands –
 There is more than glass between the snow and the huge roses.

LOUIS MACNEICE (1907-1963)

'NOW, WINTER'S DOLOROUS DAYS ARE O'ER'

*N*ow, winter's dolorous days are o'er, and through
March morning casements comes the sharp spring air,
And noises from the distant city, where
The steeples stand up keenly in the blue:
No more the clouds by crispy frost defined,
Pile the pale North, but float, dispersed shapes;
Though still around the cool grey twilight capes,
The sullen sea is dark with drifts of wind.
Like a forgotten fleck of snow still left,
The cascade gleams in the far mountain cleft;
Brown rushes by the river's brimming bank
Rustle, and matted sedges sway and sigh,
Where grasses in sleek shallows waver dank,
Or drift in windy ripples greyly by.

THOMAS CAULFIELD IRWIN (1823-1892)

Right: Muckross Lake, Co. Kerry

THE WOODS

Two years we spent
   down there, in a quaint
      outbuilding bright with recent paint.

A green retreat,
   secluded and sedate,
      part of a once great estate,

it watched our old
   bone-shaker as it growled
      with guests and groceries through heat and cold,

and heard you tocsin
   meal-times with a spoon
      while I sat working in the sun.

Above the yard
   an old clock had expired
      the night Lenin arrived in Petrograd.

Bourbons and Romanovs
   had removed their gloves
      in the drawing-rooms and alcoves

of the manor house;
   but these illustrious
      ghosts never imposed on us.

Enough that the pond
   steamed, the apples ripened,
      the conkers on the gravel opened.

continued…

Left: Portumna Castle, Co. Galway

Ragwort and hemlock,
   cinquefoil and ladysmock
      throve in the shadows at the back;

beneath the trees
   foxgloves and wood anemones
      looked up with tearful metamorphic eyes.

We woke the rooks
   on narrow, winding walks
      familiar from the story books,

or visited
   a disused garden shed
      where gas-masks from the war decayed;

and we knew peace
   splintering the thin ice
      on the bath-tub drinking-trough for cows.

But how could we
   survive indefinitely
      so far from the city and the sea?

Finding, at last,
   too creamy for our taste
      the fat profusion of that feast,

we travelled on
   to doubt and speculation,
      our birthright and our proper portion.

Another light
   than ours convenes the mute
      attention of those woods tonight –

while we, released
   from that pale paradise,
      ponder the darkness in another place.

DEREK MAHON (1941-)

PLOUGHER

*S*unset and silence! A man; around him earth savage, earth
    broken;
Beside him two horses, a plough!

Earth savage, earth broken, the brutes, the dawn-man there
    in the sunset,
And the plough that is twin to the sword, that is founder of
    cities!

'Brute-tamer, plough-maker, earth-breaker! Canst hear?
    There are ages between us –
Is it praying you are as you stand there alone in the sunset?

Surely our sky-born gods can be naught to you, earth-child
    and earth-master –
Surely your thoughts are of Pan, or of Wotan, or Dana?

Yet why give thought to the gods? Has Pan led your brutes
    where they stumble?
Has Dana numbed pain of the child-bed, or Wotan put hand
    to your plough?

What matter your foolish reply? O man standing lone and
    bowed earthward,
Your task is a day near its close. Give thanks to the night-
    giving god.'

Slowly the darkness falls, the broken lands blend with the
    savage;
The brute-tamer stands by the brutes, a head's breadth only
    above them.

A head's breadth? Aye, but therein is hell's depth and the
    height up to heaven,
And the thrones of the gods and their halls, their chariots,
    purples, and splendours.

PADRAIC COLUM (1881-1972)

DO YOU REMEMBER THAT NIGHT?

Do you remember that night
When you were at the window
With neither hat nor gloves
Nor coat to shelter you?
I reached out my hand to you
And you ardently grasped it,
I remained to converse with you
Until the lark began to sing.

Do you remember that night
That you and I were
At the foot of the rowan-tree
And the night drifting snow?
Your head on my breast,
And your pipe sweetly playing?
Little thought I that night
That our love ties would loosen!

Beloved of my inmost heart,
Come some night, and soon,
When my people are at rest,
That we may talk together.
My arms shall encircle you
While I relate my sad tale,
That your soft, pleasant converse
Hath deprived me of heaven.

The fire is unraked,
The light unextinguished,
The key under the door,
Do you softly draw it.
My mother is asleep,
But I am wide awake;
My fortune in my hand,
I am ready to go with you.

EUGENE O'CURRY (1796-1862)

Left: Winter snow on the
Dingle Peninsula

THE STRAYING STUDENT

On a holy day when sails were blowing southward,
A bishop sang the Mass at Inishmore,
Men took one side, their wives were on the other
But I heard the woman coming from the shore:
And wild in despair my parents cried aloud
For they saw the vision draw me to the doorway.

Long had she lived in Rome when Popes were bad,
The wealth of every age she makes her own,
Yet smiled on me in eager admiration,
And for a summer taught me all I know,
Banishing shame with that great laugh that rang
As if a pillar caught it back alone.

I learned the prouder counsel of her throat,
My mind was growing bold as light in Greece;
And when in sleep her stirring limbs were shown,
I blessed the noonday rock that knew no tree:
And for an hour the mountain was her throne,
Although her eyes were bright with mockery.

They say I was sent back from Salamanca
And failed in logic, but I wrote her praise
Nine times upon a college wall in France.
She laid her hand at darkfall on my page
That I might read the heavens in a glance
And I knew every star the Moors have named.

Awake or in my sleep, I have no peace now,
Before the ball is struck, my breath has gone,
And yet I tremble lest she may deceive me
And leave me in this land, where every woman's son
Must carry his own coffin and believe,
In dread, all that the clergy teach the young.

AUSTIN CLARKE (1896-1974)

101

WHEN YOU ARE OLD

When you are old and grey and full of sleep,
And nodding by the fire, take down this book,
And slowly read, and dream of the soft look
Your eyes had once, and of their shadows deep;

How many loved your moments of glad grace,
And loved your beauty with love false or true,
But one man loved the pilgrim soul in you,
And loved the sorrows of your changing face;

And bending down beside the glowing bars,
Murmur, a little sadly, how Love fled
And paced upon the mountains overhead
And hid his face amid a crowd of stars.

W.B. YEATS (1865-1939)

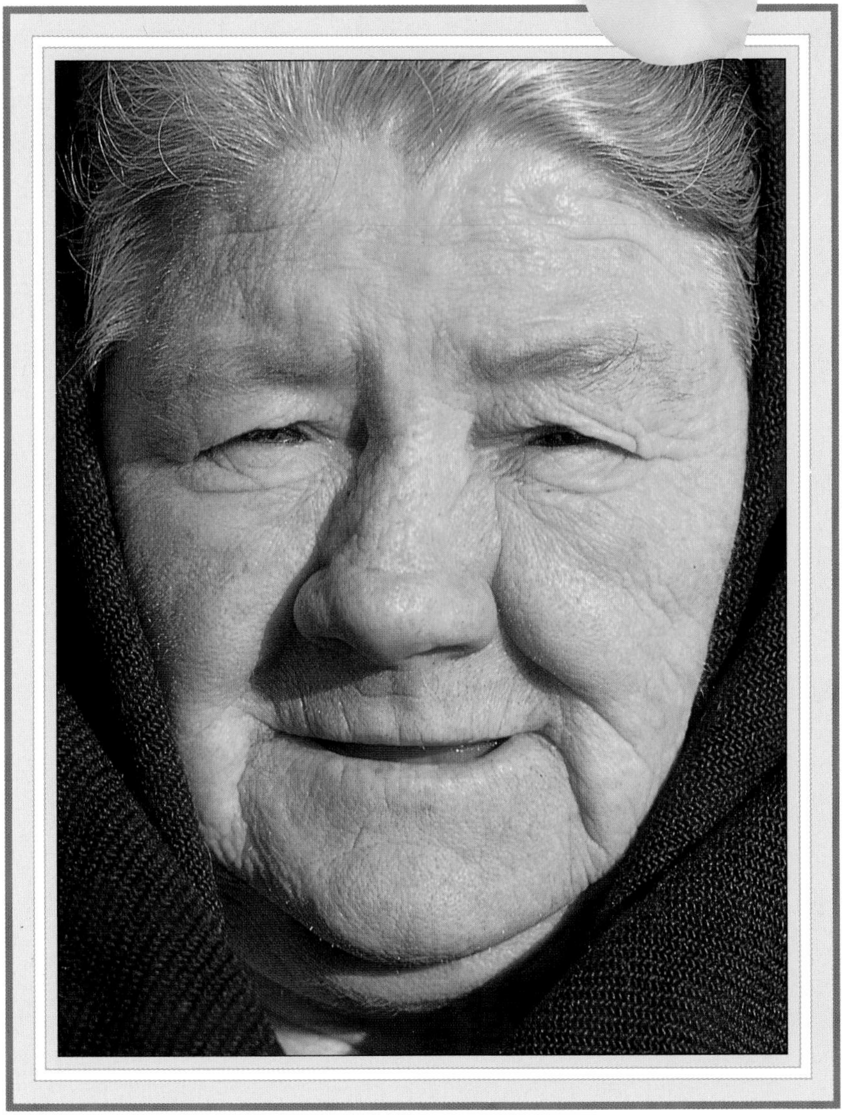

BOGLAND

for T.P. Flanagan

We have no prairies
　　To slice a big sun at evening –
Everywhere the eye concedes to
　　Encroaching horizon,

Is wooed into the cyclops' eye
　　O a tarn. Our unfenced country
Is bog that keeps crusting
　　Between the sights of the sun.

They've taken the skeleton
　　Of the Great Irish Elk
Out of the peat, set it up
　　An astounding crate full of air.

Butter sunk under
　　More than a hundred years
Was recovered salty and white.
　　The ground itself is kind, black butter

Melting and opening underfoot,
　　Missing its last definition
By millions of years.
　　They'll never dig coal here,

Only the waterlogged trunks
　　Of great firs, soft as pulp.
Our pioneers keep striking
　　Inwards and downwards,

Every layer they strip
　　Seems camped on before.
The bogholes might be Atlantic seepage.
　　The wet centre is bottomless.

SEAMUS HEANEY (1939-)

CANAL BANK WALK

Leafy-with-love banks and the green waters of the canal
Pouring redemption for me, that I do
The will of God, wallow in the habitual, the banal,
Grow with nature again as before I grew.
The bright stick trapped, the breeze adding a third
Party to the couple kissing on an old seat,
And a bird gathering materials for a nest for the Word
Eloquently new and abandoned to its delirious beat.
O unworn world enrapture me, encapture me in a web
Of fabulous grass and eternal voices by a beech,
Feed the gaping need of my senses, give me ad lib
To pray unselfconsciously with overflowing speech
For this soul needs to be honoured with a new dress woven
From green and blue things and arguments that cannot be proven

PATRICK KAVANAGH (1904-1967)

The Grand Canal, Dublin

THE VILLAGE

*S*weet was the sound, when oft at evening's close
Up yonder hill the village murmur rose;
　　There, as I passed with careless steps and slow,
　　The mingling notes came soften'd from below:
The swain responsive as the milkmaid sung,
The sober herd that low'd to meet their young;
　　The noisy geese that gabbled o'er the pool,
　　The playful children just let loose from school;
The watchdog's voice that bay'd the whisp'ring wind,
And the loud laugh that spoke the vacant mind;
　　These all in sweet confusion sought the shade,
　　And fill'd each pause the nightingale had made.
But now the sounds of population fail,
No cheerful murmurs fluctuate in the gale,
　　No busy steps the grass-grown footway tread,
　　For all the bloomy flush of life is fled.
All but yon widow'd, solitary thing,
That feebly bends beside the plashy spring:
　　She, wretched matron, forc'd in age, for bread,
　　To strip the brook with mantling cresses spread,
To strip her wintry faggot from the thorn,
To seek her nightly shed, and weep till morn;
　　She only left of all the harmless train,
　　The sad historian of the pensive plain.

OLIVER GOLDSMITH (1728-1774)

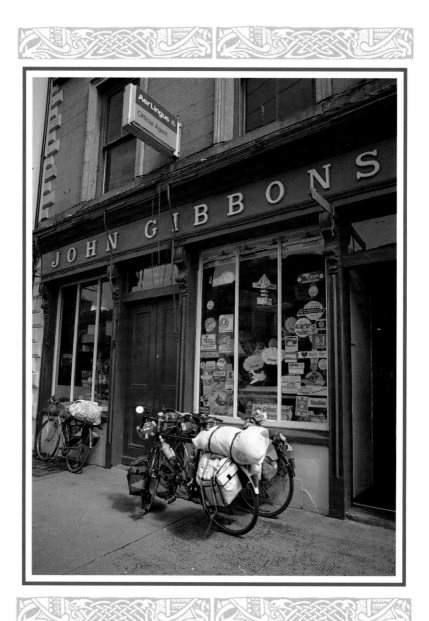

BACKSIDE TO THE WIND

A fourteen-year-old boy is out rambling alone
By the scimitar shores of Killala Bay
And he is dreaming of a French Ireland,
Backside to the wind.

What kind of village would I now be living in?
French vocabularies intertwined with Gaelic
And Irish women with French fathers,
Backsides to the wind.

The Ballina Road would become the Rue de Humbert
And wine would be the staple drink of the people;
A staple diet of potatoes and wine,
Backsides to the wind.

Monsieur O'Duffy might be the harbour-master
And Madame Duffy the mother of thirteen
Tiny philosophers to overthrow Maynooth,
Backsides to the wind.

Father Molloy might be a worker-priest
Up to his knees in manure at the cattle-mart;
And dancing and loving on the streets at evening
Backsides to the wind.

Jean Arthur Rimbaud might have grown up here
In a hillside terrace under the round tower;
Would he, like me, have dreamed of an Arabian Dublin,
Backside to the wind?

Garda Ned MacHale might now be a gendarme
Having hysterics at the crossroads;
Excommunicating male motorists, ogling females,
Backside to the wind.

continued…

I walk on, facing the village ahead of me,
A small concrete oasis in the wild countryside;
Not the embodiment of the dream of a boy,
Backside to the wind.

Seagulls and crows, priests and nuns,
Perch on the rooftops and steeples,
And their Anglo-American mores asphyxiate me,
Backside to the wind.

Not to mention the Japanese invasion:
Blunt people as serious as ourselves
And as humourless; money is our God,
Backsides to the wind.

The medieval Franciscan Friary of Moyne
Stands house-high, roofless, by;
Past it rolls a vast asphalt pipe,
Backsides to the wind,

Ferrying chemical waste out to sea
From the Asahi synthetic-fibre plant;
Where once monks sang, wage-earners slave,
Backsides to the wind.

Run on, sweet River Moy,
Although I end my song; you are
The scales of a salmon of a boy,
Backside to the wind.

Yet I have no choice but to leave, to leave,
And yet there is nowhere I more yearn to live
Than in my own wild countryside,
Backside to the wind.

PAUL DURCAN (1944-)

113

HIGH ISLAND

A shoulder of rock
Sticks high up out of the sea,
A fisherman's mark
For lobster and blue-shark.

    Fissile and stark
    The crust is flaking off,
    Seal-rock, gull-rock,
    Cove and cliff.

Dark mounds of mica schist,
A lake, mill and chapel,
Roofless, one gable smashed,
Lie ringed with rubble.

    An older calm,
    The kiss of rock and grass,
    Pink thrift and white sea-campion,
    Flowers in the dead place.

Day keeps lit a flare
Round the north pole all night
Like brushing long wavy hair
Petrels quiver in flight.

    Quietly as the rustle
    Of an arm entering a sleeve,
    They slip down to nest
    Under altar-stone or grave.

Round the wrecked laura
Needles flicker
Tacking air, quicker and quicker
To rock, sea and star.

RICHARD MURPHY (1927-)

Right: Grainnes
Wails Castle,
Achill Island

THE SWIMMER

For him the Shannon opens
Like a woman.
He has stepped over the stones

And cut the water
With his body
But this river does not bleed for

Any man. How easily
He mounts the waves, riding them
As though they

Whispered subtle invitations to his skin,
Conspiring with the sun
To offer him

A white, wet rhythm. The deep beneath
Gives full support
To the marriage of wave and heart,

The waves he breaks turn back to stare
At the repeated ceremony
And the hills of Clare

Witness the fluent weddings
The flawless congregation
The choiring foam that sings

To limbs which must, once more,
Rising and falling in the sun,
Return to shore.

Again he walks upon the stones,
A new music in his heart,
A river in his bones

Flowing forever through his head
Private as a grave
Or as the bridal bed.

BRENDAN KENNELLY (1936-)

BIRTH OF A COACHMAN

*H*is father and grandfather before him were coachmen:
How strange, then, to think that this small, bloody, lump of flesh,
    This tiny moneybags of brains, veins, and intestines,
This zipped-up purse of most peculiar coin,
    Will one day be coachman of the Cork to Dublin route,
In a great black greatcoat and white gauntlets,
    In full command of one of our famous coaches
– *Wonder*, *Perseverance*, *Diligence*, or *Lightning* –
    In charge of all our lives on foul winter nights,
Crackling his whip, whirling it, lashing it,
    Driving on the hapless horses across the moors
Of the Kilworth hills, beating them on
    Across rivers in spate, rounding sharp bends
On only two wheels, shrieking of axle-trees,
    Rock-scrapes, rut-squeals, quagmire-squelches,
For ever in dread of the pitiless highwayman
    Lurking in ambush with a brace of pistols;
Then cantering carefully in the lee of the Galtees,
    Bowing his head to the stone gods of Cashel;
Then again thrusting through Urlingford;
    Doing his bit, and his nut, past the Devilsbit;
Praising the breasts of the hills round Port Laoise;
    Sailing full furrow through the Curragh of Kildare,
Through the thousand sea-daisies of a thousand white sheep;
    Thrashing gaily the air at first glimpse of the Liffey;
Until stepping down from his high perch in Dublin
    Into the sanctuary of a cobbled courtyard,
Into the arms of a crowd like a triumphant toreador
    All sweat and tears: the man of the moment
Who now is but a small body of but some fleeting seconds old.

PAUL DURCAN (1944-)

Left: The Gap of Dunloe, Co. Kerry

MY DARK FATHERS

*M*y dark fathers lived the intolerable day
Committed always to the night of wrong,
    Stiffened at the heartstone, the woman lay,
    Perished feet nailed to her man's breastbone.
Grim houses beckoned in the swelling gloom
Of Munster fields where the Atlantic night
    Fettered the child within the pit of doom,
    And everywhere a going down of light.

And yet upon the sandy Kerry shore
The woman once had danced at ebbing tide
    Because she loved flute music – and still more
    Because a lady wondered at the pride
Of one so humble. That was long before
The green plants withered by an evil chance;
    When winds of hunger howled at every door
    She heard the music dwindle and forgot the dance.

Such mercy as the wolf receives was hers
Whose dance became a rhythm in a grave,
    Achieved beneath the thorny savage furze
    That yellowed fiercely in a mountain cave.
Immune to pity, she, whose crime was love,
Crouched, shivered, searched the threatening sky,
    Discovered ready signs, compelled to move
    Her to her innocent appalling cry.

continued…

Inch Beach,
Co. Kerry

Skeletoned in darkness, my dark fathers lay
Unknown, and could not understand
    The giant grief that trampled night and day,
    The awful absence moping through the land.
Upon the headland, the encroaching sea
Left sand that hardened after tides of Spring,
    No dancing feet disturbed its symmetry
    And those who loved good music ceased to sing.

Since every moment of the clock
Accumulates to form a final name,
    Since I am come of Kerry clay and rock,
    I celebrate the darkness and the shame
That could compel a man to turn his face
Against the wall, withdrawn from light so strong
    And undeceiving, spancelled in a place
    Of unapplauding hands and broken song.

BRENDAN KENNELLY (1936-)

THE MEETING OF THE WATERS

There is not in the wide world a valley so sweet
As that vale in whose bosom the bright waters meet;
Oh! the last rays of feeling and life must depart,
Ere the bloom of that valley shall fade from my heart.

Yet it *was* not that Nature had shed o'er the scene
Her purest of crystal and brightest of green;
'Twas *not* her soft magic of streamlet or hill,
Oh! no, – it was something more exquisite still.

'Twas that friends, the belov'd of my bosom, were near,
Who made every dear scene of enchantment more dear,
And who felt how the best charms of nature improve,
When we see them reflected from looks that we love.

Sweet vale of Avoca! how calm could I rest
In thy bosom of shade, with the friends I love best,
Where the storms that we feel in this cold world should cease,
And our hearts, like thy waters, be mingled in peace.

THOMAS MOORE (1779-1852)

GATHERING MUSHROOMS

The rain comes flapping through the yard
like a tablecloth that she hand-embroidered.
My mother has left it on the line.
It is sodden with rain,
The mushroom shed is windowless, wide,
its high-stacked mushroom trays
hosed down with formaldehyde.
And my father has opened the Gates of Troy
to that first load of horse manure.
Barley straw. Gypsum. Dried blood. Ammonia.
Wagon after wagon
blusters in, a self-renewing gold-black dragon
we push to the back of the mind.
We have taken our pitchforks to the wind.

All brought back to me that September evening
fifteen years on. The pair of us
tripping through Barnett's fair demesne
like girls in long dresses
after a hail-storm.
We might have been thinking of the fire-bomb
that sent Malone House sky-high
and its priceless collection of linen
sky-high.
We might have wept with Elizabeth McCrum.
We were thinking only of psilocobyn.
You sang of the maid you met on the dewy grass –
And she stooped so low gave me to know
it was mushrooms she was gathering O.

continued...

He'll be wearing that same old donkey-jacket
and the sawn-off waders.
He carries a knife, two punnets, a bucket.
He reaches far into his own shadow.
We'll have taken him unawares
and stand behind him, slightly to one side.
He is one of those ancient warriors
before the rising tide.
He'll glance back from under his peaked cap
without breaking rhythm:
his coaxing a mushroom – a flat or a cup –
the nick against his right thumb;
the bucket then, the punnet to left or right,
and so on and so forth till kingdom come.

We followed the overgrown tow-path by the Lagan.
The sunset would deepen through cinnamon
to aubergine,
the wood-pigeon's concerto for oboe and strings,
allegro, blowing your mind.
And you were suddenly out of my ken, hurtling
towards the ever-receding ground,
into the maw
of a shimmering green-gold dragon.
You discovered yourself in some outbuilding
with your long-lost companion, me,
though my head had grown into the head of a horse
that shook its dirty-fair mane
and spoke this verse:

Come back to us. However cold and raw, your feet
were always meant
to negotiate terms with bare cement.
Beyond this concrete wall is a wall of concrete
and barbed wire. Your only hope
is to come back. If sing you must, let your song
tell of treading your own dung,
let straw and dung give a spring to your step.
If we never live to see the day we leap
into our true domain,
lie down with us now and wrap
yourself in the soiled grey blanket of Irish rain
that will, one day, bleach itself white.
Lie down with us and wait.

(PAUL MULDOON 1951-)

129
~

LINES WRITTEN ON A SEAT ON THE GRAND CANAL, DUBLIN, 'ERECTED TO THE MEMORY OF MRS DERMOT O'BRIEN'

O commemorate me where there is water,
Canal water preferably, so stilly
Greeny at the heart of summer. Brother
Commemorate me thus beautifully
Where by a lock Niagarously roars
The falls for those who sit in the tremendous silence
Of mid-July. No one will speak in prose
Who finds his way to these Parnassian islands.
A swan goes by head low with many apologies,
Fantastic light looks through the eyes of bridges –
And look! a barge comes bringing from Athy
And other far-flung towns mythologies.
O commemorate me with no hero-courageous
Tomb – just a canal-bank seat for the passer-by.

PATRICK KAVANAGH (1904-1967)

Right: The Grand Canal, Dublin

I SAW FROM THE BEACH

I saw from the beach, when the morning was shining,
    A bark o'er the waters move gloriously on;
I came when the sun from that beach was declining,
    The bark was still there, but the waters were gone.

And such is the fate of our life's early promise,
    So passing the spring-tide of joy we have known;
Each wave, that we danc'd on at morning, ebbs from us,
    And leaves us, at eve, on the bleak shore alone.

Ne'er tell me of glories, serenely adorning
    The close of our day, the calm eve of our night; –
Give me back, give me back the wild freshness of Morning,
    Her clouds and her tears are worth Evening's best light.

THOMAS MOORE (1779-1852)

RED HANRAHAN'S SONG ABOUT IRELAND

The old brown thorn-trees break in two high over Cummen Strand,
Under a bitter black wind that blows from the left hand;
Our courage breaks like an old tree in a black wind and dies,
But we have hidden in our hearts the flame out of the eyes
Of Cathleen, the daughter of Houlihan.

The wind has bundled up the clouds high over Knocknarea,
And thrown the thunder on the stones for all that Maeve can say.
Angers that are like noisy clouds have set our hearts abeat;
But we have all bent low and low and kissed the quiet feet
Of Cathleen, the daughter of Houlihan.

The yellow pool has overflowed high up on Clooth-na-Bare,
For the wet winds are blowing out of the clinging air;
Like heavy flooded waters our bodies and our blood;
But purer than a tall candle before the Holy Rood
Is Cathleen, the daughter of Houlihan.

W.B. YEATS (1865-1939)

Right: Curraheen River, Co. Kerry

INDEX OF FIRST LINES

ACKNOWLEDGEMENTS

Acknowledgement is made by the publishers to the following for permission
to reprint the poems in this treasury:

'High Island' from *New selected Poems* by Richard Murphy (Faber and Faber); 'Bogland'
and 'The Forge' from *Door into the Dark* by Seamus Heaney (Faber and Faber); 16 lines
from 'At a Potato Digging' from *Death of a Naturalist* by Seamus Heaney (Faber and
Faber); 'The Avenue' from *Why Brownlee Left* by Paul Muldoon (Faber and Faber);
'Gathering Mushrooms' from *Quoof* by Paul Muldoon (Faber and Faber); 'The Swimmer'
and 'My Dark Fathers' reprinted by permission of Bloodaxe Books Ltd from *A Time for
Voices: Selected Poems 1960-1990* by Brendan Kennelly (Bloodaxe Books, 1990); 'The
Limerick Train' by Brendan Kennelly reprinted by permission of Bloodaxe Books; 'Achill'
by Derek Mahon , from *Antarctica* © 1985, by permission of The Gallery Press,
Loughcrew, Oldcastle, Co. Meath, Ireland; 'October', 'Canal Bank Walk' and 'Lines
Written on a Seat on the Grand Canal' by Patrick Kavanagh, reprinted by permission of
the trustees of the estate of Patrick Kavanagh, c/o Peter Fallon, Literary Agent,
Loughcrew, Oldcastle, Co. Meath, Ireland; 'In Carrowdore Churchyard' from *Poems 1962-
1978* by Derek Mahon, reprinted by permission of Oxford University Press; 'The Woods'
from *The Hunt by Night* by Derek Mahon, reprinted by permission of Oxford University
Press; 'Plougher', 'An Old Woman of the Roads' and 'She Moved Through the Fair' from
The Poet's Circuits by Padraic Colum (Dolmen Press, 1981), reprinted by permission of the
estate of Padraic Colum; 'Snow', 'Sunlight on the Garden' and 'House on a Cliff' from
Collected Poems by Louis MacNeice (Faber and Faber), by permission of David Higham
Associates Ltd; 'September 1913', 'The Lake Isle of Innisfree', 'When You are Old', 'He
Wishes for the Cloths of Heaven', 'In the Seven Woods' and 'Red Hanrahan's Song about
Ireland' by W.B.Yeats, reprinted courtesy of Macmillan London; 'The Straying Student',
'Martha Blake' and 'Her Voice Could not be Safer' from *Collected Poems* by Austin Clarke
(Dolmen Press 1974), reprinted by permission of R. Dardis Clarke and Lilliput Press;
'After the Irish of Egan O'Rahilly' by Eavan Boland, reprinted by kind
permission of the author